AUDACIOUS GENEROSITY

AUDACIOUS
GENEROSITY

HOW TO EXPERIENCE,
RECEIVE, AND GIVE
MORE THAN YOU EVER
THOUGHT POSSIBLE

KEVIN WHITE

AUDACIOUS GENEROSITY

How to Experience, Receive, and Give More
Than You Ever Thought Possible

ISBN   978-1-5445-1615-8 *Hardcover*
       978-1-5445-1614-1 *Paperback*
       978-1-5445-1613-4 *Ebook*
       978-1-6649-4236-3 *Audiobook*

To the estimated three billion precious men, women, boys, and girls worldwide who still have limited access to know about Jesus.

To the Believers worldwide who are living intentionally every day to fulfill the Great Commission.

CONTENTS

A WORD FROM KEVIN'S FAMILY

Audacious Generosity is an experience, a movement of God. As God began the work of generosity in my life and Kevin's life, my heart was much like the widow of Zarephath. Elijah came to her and asked her to bake for him and then for her and her son. The widow responded, "as the Lord lives I only have a handful, and we will surely die if I use it to bake for you." My heart was afraid like the widow, but as we gave, our jars began overflowing—we had to give more away because there was so much! Audacious Generosity will move you to find the places of surrender in your life and let God do the impossible! I'm grateful Kevin led our family in audacious generosity in little and in much.

—SHELLY WHITE, KEVIN'S WIFE

Growing up generously wasn't always easy but watching my dad and mom model God's love to others, and seeing God provide for His Children in need, taught me as a child why it is more blessed to give than receive. God always provided, and many times gave us gifts ten times more abundant than we deserved, that were physical and memorable...but the greatest gift was letting me see Him love His people firsthand. Now twenty years later, I still see the effects of God working in our family by us committing to live generously!

—ZACH WHITE, SON, AGE THIRTY

It has been such a blessing to have Kevin and Shelly play a crucial role in my relationship with their son. From the early stages of dating to our one-year anniversary of marriage, they have faithfully prayed for and over us, encouraged us, and asked probing questions to make sure our relationship with God is strongest above all. In every decision we've made, they've been there to remind us of God's faithfulness and generosity—as long as we are open and willing to receive it and give in return.

—BRITTANY WHITE, ZACH'S WIFE

My parents, Kevin and Shelly, not only taught us to be like Jesus, they actively lived lives of audacious generosity. When our family lost our home, I only remember instances of God providing for every single need we represented...and then I watched God provide for thousands of other families through us. You won't know how much God cares for you until you allow Him to use you to love others well. Audacious Generosity is a heart posture.

—KOURTNEY WHITE, DAUGHTER, AGE TWENTY-SEVEN

When I was a kid, I was confused by why we had to give our things away. Now, as an adult, I realize my parents were setting an example of Jesus' love. God always exceeds our expectations when we open our hands and allow Him to use what we have. I encourage everyone to experience the freedom found in being audaciously generous!

KALI WHITE, DAUGHTER, AGE TWENTY-FIVE

INTRODUCTION

GOD'S STRATEGY HAS ALWAYS BEEN AUDACIOUS GENEROSITY

We all have an innate desire to be more generous but don't know how. When it comes to the subject of giving, most of us feel like we have nothing left to give.

What's worse? Our fear of failure then keeps us from being generous.

Unfortunately, most of us have no margin in our life for generosity. We are maxed out financially. We are already overbooked. It is all we can do to hold our own lives together. The Great Commission Jesus gives us in Matthew 28:18-20 is our last priority.

I know this from personal experience.

If you have ever felt pressured to give, then you have been made to think that you are the giver and that giving depends on what you can produce. I know the frustration that comes from the endless sense that we ought to give more without a clear path of how to become more generous. I also know the fear that giving now could result in the humiliation of complete financial ruin later.

But it doesn't have to be that way. In fact, through my own experiences, I know a better way—through God's strategy of audacious generosity.

But what does that mean? John 3:16 says, "For God so loved the world that He gave Jesus." God's plan has always been Jesus and His strategy has always been audacious generosity.

Let's define audacious generosity. "Audacious" is an adjective describing a willingness to take surprisingly bold risks. "Generosity" is a noun identifying the quality of being kind and plentiful. Now, putting the two together:

Audacious generosity is a willingness to take surprisingly bold risks by being kind and plentiful.

This is an attribute of God we see demonstrated throughout Scripture.

We all have an innate desire to be more and give more. We sincerely want to help other people to survive and thrive too. The problem is we have learned to avoid the subject of giving. Think about it: How many people do you know who wake up every morning excited to be more generous? I'm willing to guess it's not very many.

Jesus promises that it is more blessed to give than to receive. In the pages that follow, I will uncover those blessings of God that result only from giving through His strategy of audacious generosity. This book will help you exchange any sense of pressure and regret for genuine confidence and satisfaction, and give you the real encouragement you need to live generously.

REAL ENCOURAGEMENT

"Encouragement" is a noun describing the action of giving someone confidence. The word encourage comes from the Old French word *encoragier*, meaning to "make strong." Courage results in freedom, and when you combine courage and freedom, you get audacious generosity. I've allocated two whole chapters to courage. By the end of the book, you will be "in courage," and courage will be in you. If there is anything the world needs today, it is more courage.

Encouragement also means the persuasion to go the right way. By the end of the book, you will not only see that audacious generosity is the right way to go, but you will also know exactly how to get there.

God has scripted something much bigger for your life than for you to just survive until you go to heaven. Just in case you need encouragement to lower your guard, let me quickly tell you three things audacious generosity is NOT:

1. Audacious generosity is not about beating you up for not giving.
2. Audacious generosity is not about pressuring you to give what you can produce.
3. Audacious generosity is not about getting you to give with entitlement for personal gain.

Let me make it clear, audacious generosity is about you allowing God room in your life to do exceedingly more than you can ask or imagine (Ephesians 3:20). It is not about us bossing God around or our faith being some force that guarantees prosperity.

Audacious generosity is about your life on earth counting in heaven. It's about you allowing God to use you to bring heaven to earth. We don't have to look far to agree that we certainly need more of heaven on earth right now. Audacious generosity is also about you taking as many people as possible to heaven with you.

Audacious generosity is where God is the Giver and giving depends on what God puts into your hands. I want you to see what happens when you commit to living openhandedly before God, ready to use what He puts into your hands to fulfill His mission, and watch your relationship with Him come alive as He gives through you.

God uses audacious generosity to totally transform how you see Him, yourself, and others. As a result of reading *Audacious Generosity,* you can have a life empowered for limitless giving. Your life can be filled with a sense of completeness, satisfaction, and excitement.

When you finish reading this book, the goal is for you to enjoy a living relationship with God that's fueled by courage, characterized by freedom, and overflowing with audacious generosity. As God combines courage and freedom in your life, you will experience, receive, and give more than you ever thought possible.

THREE STEPS TOWARD AUDACIOUS GENEROSITY

The book is divided into three sections. Each section represents a significant step we must take in order to enjoy a life of audacious generosity:

1. Setting God free
2. Setting yourself free

3. Setting others free

Each section contains three specific points of encouragement that guide you in taking each step. I conclude each section with practical applications.

It is my prayer that reading this book will become a worshipful encounter with God for you. I strongly recommend you use a journal to record significant things God says as you read. It is amazing how God will speak and guide us when we value what He says enough to write it down. I also hope you'll underline, dog-ear, and mark up your book however you need to make it stick. I pray you'll look back and see this as a spiritual marker of God's transformation in your life.

FROM WANTING TO DIE TO WANTING TO GIVE

I gave my life to Christ when I was ten years old. Twenty years later, after being fired from a church for being an insecure workaholic for God, I actually regretted becoming a Christian. The pressure I put on myself to produce and give was killing every area of my life. I wanted to die.

That's when God took me more than 8,000 miles away and used India to change my life. On the plane ride back, I committed to making my life's mission to passionately pursue the presence of God. During the next few years, God gave me the courage and freedom to let go of what I could produce, which is tiny, in order to receive what He can produce, which is limitless.

As you'll read, this included everything down to our house, automobiles, and personal belongings. I started living openhandedly before God. Miracles started happening as I recognized God as the Giver. Something released in heaven as I committed in advance to use what God put into my hands to fulfill His mission on earth. All of a sudden, giving meant simply RELEASING what God put into my hands.

This has continued for over twenty years. Today I experience, receive, and give more than I ever thought possible. Just wait until you hear some of the miracles we've witnessed God perform in our very own hands. But I can take no credit. It has all been Christ working through me.

The surprising thing is the more I give, the more I receive. I seek to always give God my everything. I have firsthand experience that it is impossible to outgive God. He is so faithful, loving, kind, and plentiful. Now, it is my high honor to be a Christian and to enjoy this life of audacious generosity. I wake up every morning wanting to be more generous than I was the day before.

It saddens me how the vast majority of my brothers and sisters in Christ identify more with my first twenty years of Christian bondage than they do the last twenty years of audacious generosity. I want to change that. Together, we are going to change audacious generosity from being the exception to being the norm for ALL followers of Christ.

For over twenty years, God has had me staring at the 1.3 billion Indian Nationals who desperately need to know about Jesus. India alone represents one-third of all people far from God without access to hear about Jesus. Every day, 25,000 Indian Nationals die without knowing Jesus, only to face a Christless eternity. That's 9,125,000 people a year. That's a staggering number for me, but I have found that most people are completely unaware of this.

Audacious generosity is a movement where Believers around the world unite to fulfill the Great Commission. It's believing everyone ought to have access to hear about Jesus. And, it's taking action to do something about it.

LIVE WITH AUDACIOUS GENEROSITY

Audacious generosity will show you how to set God, yourself, and others free. At the end of this book, I will be issuing a simple yet profound call to action so you can start living with audacious generosity right away. Change won't happen overnight, but by starting with small practices, you can start opening your hands up to God. I hope you're excited. I am.

I'd like to pray for you:

Heavenly Father, I ask that every person holding this book will be given a stronger sense of Your presence in their life. Let them passionately pursue Your presence first and foremost. Father, give them grace every day to ask You for more. Give them grace to take courage, find freedom, and to experience You give through them with audacious generosity. I pray they will begin to experience, receive, and give more than they ever thought possible. I pray that they will allow You to be free to be who You say You are and to do what You say You will do. I pray that they will really and completely set You, themselves, and others free. Father, may the love You have for the world overflow in them. Let the same miracles they read about in Your Word be witnessed today with their own eyes as You perform Your miracles in their hands. In Jesus' name, Amen.

Buckle up. The first step of setting God free requires God-sized courage. The good news is that courage is already waiting for you.

SECTION 1

SET GOD FREE

CHAPTER 1

LIVE RECKLESSLY TO EXPERIENCE MORE

Asking God for food for others seemed like a reckless act of inconsideration to our family.

It was the year 2000, and I found myself living on less than $500 a month in Cary, North Carolina, with my wife Shelly, our three young children, and a foster son. For two years prior, I had been serving with a local counseling ministry to pastors, and two men in our church had been underwriting the bulk of our monthly support.

One of the men supporting our ministry left the church, and we began to face severe financial hardship. Despite working full time in the ministry, our income suddenly dropped to less than $500 per month. Eventually, it got to the point when there was no food in the cabinets. I did what anyone would do: I began praying and looking for work.

This was one of the hardest experiences of my life. It was a daily mix of gore and glory. I use "gore" to describe the reality of life being messy and hard at times. I use "glory" to describe the reality of God's presence and the peace of God that transcends human understanding. In my quiet time, I could always find peace in the presence of God, but every time I looked for work, the peace left. This went on for weeks. I filled up journals with specific Scriptures God gave me to give me strength. I had no money, but I was free from fear.

I remember how perplexing it was for our brothers and sisters in Christ to watch us go through it. I applied for dozens of minimum wage jobs and would have gladly flipped burgers or done janitorial work, but I didn't receive any job offers. The unemployment rate was low, and there was no earthly reason why I couldn't find a job. I began to see there was a heavenly reason, though. Shelly and I confronted the reality head-on that God's ways are higher than ours (Isaiah 55:8-9). There is no way I would have ever chosen to go through this. Yet, I'd do it all over again because of the value it gave me for God's presence and the miracles that are still occurring as a result.

I don't know how many times a day I humbled myself before God asking for guidance. It was like the fiery furnace we read about in Daniel 3. The presence of God was so real, and we never smelled burnt from the flames. God was with us.

God gave me new words to pray: "Father, give us food that others might eat." As I was in the Word, I kept reading Matthew 6:33, "Seek the Kingdom of God above all else, and live righteously, and he will give you everything you need," (NLT). The closer we got to having no food, the more compassion God gave me for hungry people who didn't know the hope we had been given. For days, the Spirit guided me to look at the miracle of the Feeding of the Multitude in John 6:1-15. God began impressing upon me: "You can feed your family, but only I can feed the multitude." I just kept praying, "Father, give us food that others might eat."

One morning, I went to a local grocery store with about four dollars in my pocket. I was looking over their discounted meats so our family could eat that day. I was walking up the soft drink aisle and saw a store employee coming toward me. Without any prior thought, I stopped her and found out she was the deli manager. "Excuse me, what do you do with your expired products?" I asked.

"We throw them away," she said.

"Would you be open to me taking it and giving it to families in need?"

"Come back tomorrow, and I will ask the store manager."

I went back the next day, found the deli manager, and she immediately pointed to three grocery carts full of rotisserie chicken, pizza, pasta, and everything the deli and bakery sold. The shelf life had expired, but it was perfectly edible. "Take it," she said.

"How do I take it?" I asked.

"Roll it right out through the front doors of the store. I've cleared it with the manager." I remember waiting for someone to stop me as I rolled the three carts past the cash registers and right out the front of the store, but no one said anything. I even grabbed a big stack of grocery bags. The food filled my Toyota sedan from top to bottom, barely leaving enough room for me to drive home.

Oh, you should have seen it. When I pulled up, the kids ran around the car, rejoicing as I assured Shelly I hadn't just robbed a grocery store. We filled the refrigerator and every cabinet in our house to give to others. The next day it happened again. Then the next. We quickly realized the clock is ticking just like with the manna and quail in Exodus 16. God taught us:

Hoard it and lose it. Give it, and it returns.

We started looking everywhere to find people who needed food. Within a few days, we had identified needy families in our community with whom we could bless with a bag of groceries. Soon the word got out, and a distribution schedule was established so that no food was wasted.

One year later, we were feeding five hundred needy families per month with the help of twenty-five volunteer families. God had led us to freely give it all away free through a ministry called With Love from Jesus. And our family of six never missed a meal.

That's how With Love from Jesus Ministries in Raleigh, North Carolina, began. Every year for the last twenty years, God has used hundreds of Believers from over fifty local churches to distribute millions of dollars in food and needed resources to high-need populations and to see thousands of lives transformed by the gospel of Jesus Christ.

But none of that would have happened if I didn't set God free and witness His audacious generosity through me.

STEP #1: SET GOD FREE

The first step toward audacious generosity is setting God free. The story I just shared describes the time I learned the need and value of setting God free. Let me highlight a few adjustments I had to make in order to do that. God led me to:

1. Prioritize His presence above everything else in my life.
2. Trust our needs to Him in order to focus instead on others who need His presence.
3. Shift my focus from receiving to giving.
4. Shift my dependency from what I can produce to what God can produce.
5. Open my hands to Him.
6. Commit in advance to use what He puts in my hands for His mission.

These resulted in setting God free in my life and opened the door to His audacious generosity through me.

The concept of setting God free receives two very predominant responses. The first is, "Well, duh." The second is, "How dare you!" Few things cause more resistance among Christians than this concept of us setting God free. Some Christians even suggest it is heresy to say we need to set God free.

Allow me to explain. By setting God free, I'm simply talking about our need to let God be God. It is us relinquishing full control over to Him. We let Him call the shots. We let Him guide us in ways that seem illogical to us. We believe He is who He says He is and will do what He says He will do. We grant Him access to all areas of our life. We set God free to be God.

I'm not suggesting we can somehow override the sovereignty of God. The same people who resist the concept of setting God free will have no difficulty telling us that if we visit a pornographic website that we're opening our lives up to Satan. Why accept that we can give Satan freedom to work in our lives, but reject that we can give God freedom to work in our lives? I'm telling you right now, until God is set free in your life, audacious generosity is not possible.

Research shows that 2.3 billion people worldwide identify as Christians. Evidence is showing that God is being restrained more than He is being set free among His people. The increase in depression, divorce, debt, and discrimination, along with the decrease in generosity—specifically the giving to missions—are all major indicators of our need to set God free.

When God is set free, His values increase, not decrease. The Bible makes it clear God values our wellness, unity, generosity, and the Great Commission. When God is set free, the courage and freedom only He can provide should show forth in confidence and generosity through His people.

When Mary said, "May it be to me as you have said" (Luke 1:38), she was setting God free. When the disciples dropped their nets and followed Jesus in Mark 1:18, they were setting God free. In Luke 21:2 when the widow dropped in her two last coins while the rich gave a tiny portion of their surplus, she was setting God free.

Each example represents:

1. God-sized courage in order to join the mission of God.
2. Freedom to hear and obey the voice of God.
3. Major adjustments they had to make in order to set God free.
4. Audacious generosity for God. Mary gave her body. The disciples gave their lives and careers. The widow gave everything.

What about you? Can you identify how you dropped your nets? Gave God your body? Gave Him everything? Have you set God free?

Here are simple questions to identify if you have set God free:

1. Is God free to speak to you? Can He say anything at anytime because you're listening expectantly?
2. Is God free to be Father, Son, and Holy Spirit any way He wants in your life?
3. Is God free to guide you into His Word? As you read God's Word, do you hear Him speaking to you?
4. Is God free to pray His prayers through you, no matter how audacious or in what language?
5. Is God free to own you and your possessions? Is He free to give and take away however He chooses?
6. Is God free to direct your giving, spending, and savings?

7. Is God free to guide you to empty your pockets and bank accounts if He wanted?
8. Is God free to make you look foolish?
9. Is God free to disappoint you? Confuse you? Frustrate you?
10. Is God free to tell you where to go and what to do?
11. Is God free to work through you to fulfill His mission?
12. Is God free to be generous (kind and plentiful) through you?

This is not meant to condemn or defeat you. Let it provide practical ways we are to set God free. If the answer to any of these questions is no, then God needs to be set free. The point is that trying to control God and living with audacious generosity don't mix.

All of us want our lives to be meaningful and impactful. Taking Jesus only for salvation is honoring Him as Savior. This opens the door to a living relationship with God. As this relationship grows, we soon recognize that Jesus is Savior and Lord. It has been well said Jesus isn't Lord at all until He is Lord of all. Another way to understand Jesus as Lord is to let Jesus become the Master of our life.

God wants to be Master in order to GIVE us a mission—His mission. As soon as Jesus says, "Come follow me" (Matthew 4:19), He immediately says, "Go" (Mark 16:15). It took me the longest time to realize that the mission of God is a

GIFT, not a CURSE. God GIVES us His mission to make our life meaningful and impactful. The reason He wants to be recognized as Master is that He knows we need a mission for our life. Stay with me.

MISSION PLUS STRATEGY FUELS GENEROSITY

Research shows that generosity is on the decline. In section 3, I provide current research relevant to generosity. For now, let me summarize how research is showing younger generations consider themselves more generous than previous generations, but they are giving substantially less. Eighty percent of Christians give less than $50 per year to the church. Giving to missions is down by 50 percent since 1990.

I want to help you make two critical connections. The first one is that **our lack of generosity results from our lack of mission.** I know this from personal experience.

When God was impressing upon me, "You can feed your family, but only I can feed the multitude," He wasn't saying that family and career aren't valuable. He was shifting my focus. Taking care of myself and my family focuses my attention on RECEIVING. Taking on God's mission focuses my attention on GIVING. This is where the greater blessings are found. Jesus promises it is more blessed to GIVE than to RECEIVE.

It is God's mission that brings fulfillment and satisfaction into your life. You have the capacity to feed your family. Only God can feed the multitudes. It is His mission that gets your focus off of yourself. It is His mission that forces your dependency off of the portion you can produce, and on to the miraculous portion God can produce. It is His mission that allows Him to perform miracles through you.

> The difference between giving from what we produce and giving from what God produces is audacious generosity.

Here is a crash course on the mission of God: Since Adam and Eve rebelled against God, we have all been born with a problem called sin (Romans 3:23). This sin of rebelling against God keeps us from a Holy God (Romans 6:23). Fortunately, God had a plan named Jesus (John 3:16). For God so loved the world that He gave Jesus to die on the cross in our place for the forgiveness of our sin. Jesus was crucified, buried, and rose again on the third day, proving He alone holds the keys to life and death (1 Corinthians 15). Now, you and I have a choice (John 1:12). Take Jesus only for Salvation or face a Christless eternity in a horrible place called hell (Romans 6:23).

The whole world means the *whole* world. God wishes none should perish and all would come to repentance (2 Peter 3:9). Before returning to the Father, Jesus gathered His followers and said, "I have been given all authority in heaven and on earth. Therefore, go and make disciples of all the nations, baptizing them in the name of the Father and the Son and the Holy Spirit. Teach these new disciples to obey all the commands I have given you. And be sure of this: I am with you always, even to the end of the age" (Matthew 28:18-20 NLT). And this, my friend, is the mission of God. Many refer to it as "the Great Commission."

In Matthew 24:14, Jesus says, "This gospel of the kingdom will be preached in the whole world as a testimony to all nations, and then the end will come," (NIV). So here is where we stand. Over seven billion people are alive today. Roughly four billion have access to hear the good news about Jesus. This leaves three billion people who still have limited to no access today to hear about Him.

The vast majority of these people far from God live in what is referred to as the "10/40 Window." This is the rectangular area of North Africa, the Middle East, and Asia approximately between ten degrees north and forty degrees north latitude. India sits in the middle of the 10/40 Window. India is just one of the three billion precious souls in this part of the world without access to hear about Jesus. For example, in the USA, there is one Believer for every 1.5 people. In India, there is one Believer for every 18,000 people. Most Christians and people with access to hear about Jesus are taking no measurable action to make Christ known to these people far from God.

God's mission has always been to extend His presence on the whole earth. He has a plan named Jesus, and His strategy has always been audacious generosity.

The second connection I want to help you make is that **our lack of generosity results from our lack of strategy.** The challenge is that most Believers have never taken the opportunity to accept audacious generosity as their strategy. When we trust Jesus for salvation, we are born again of the Holy Spirit. We become a beneficiary of God's audacious generosity. We don't just experience audacious generosity. We actually receive God's own characteristic of audacious generosity within us as we are filled with the Holy Spirit. God's audacious generosity is now within us.

God is the owner of all things. This is the God who dwells within us. We are talking about the most generous person in the world.

As a Christian, you have the richest and most generous person living inside of you.

He is able to do so much more than take care of you. He's got your back. You are secure.

What about those who don't yet have their hope in God? Who has their backs? Where do they find the peace, love, and grace you have been shown?

You and I have the opportunity to give more than we ever thought possible.

The richest and most generous person living inside us lacks nothing to give to them except our availability to let Him do it through us.

In *Audacious Generosity*, we see God is the Master Giver. I need you to hear this loud and clear: God is NOT dependent on what you can give to Him. You are dependent on what He can give you. You will never know true fulfillment and satisfaction in life until you allow God as the Master of your life to give you a mission for your life. Your mission has always been and will always be to passionately pursue the presence of God.

Nothing has illuminated the presence of God in my life like audacious generosity. The sole reason He put breath in your lungs is so that you will enjoy a living relationship with Him. As this happens, you will be confronted with your need to set Him free in your life. Free to exchange your values with His values, your motives with His motives, your mission with His mission.

Here's the kicker: The mission of God is so massive it will completely overwhelm you unless you understand His strategy and how He backs up His strategy. Right here is where a lot of Christians stop setting God free. It is one thing to accept God as Master. It is another thing to agree with the Mission of God. It is an entirely different thing to accept God's strategy for fulfilling His mission.

Every one of us has felt pressured to give. We've all been made to think giving depends on what we could produce. We look at God's giant mission in front of us, we look at our resources, and we say, "No way." And then we put God back in a box. Moving forward, we avoid the subject of giving. We return our focus to taking care of ourselves. Oh, we pray for God's mission to be fulfilled, but we don't join the mission. This limits our experience of God, our relationship with God stalls, and our lives fill up with regret.

Audacious generosity is where God is the Giver, and giving depends on what God gives through you. Audacious generosity depends on what God can produce, not what you can produce.

WHY AUDACIOUS GENEROSITY?

Nothing makes the gospel more attractive than audacious generosity. The result of God giving through you is a very practical experience with God. Nothing has impacted me more about God than the reality that he is so practical.

To the hungry, He is food.
To the naked, He is clothing.

To the lonely, He is a friend.

To the cold, He is warmth.

To the depressed, He is hope.

To the sick, He is the healer.

To the prisoner, He is freedom.

To the scared, He is peace.

To the unwise, He is wisdom.

To the lost, He is a mission.

To the guilty, He is forgiveness.

To the fearful, He is security.

To the rejected, He is acceptance.

To the houseless, He is a home.

To the fatherless, He is a father.

To the demon-possessed, He is authority.

To the racist, He is love.

To the greedy, He is generosity.

I've witnessed this for over twenty years in India through my work in Global Hope India. I've seen God work in the hearts of Hindus and Muslims as the Christian Church provided free medical clinics, clean-water projects, children's programs, employable-skills training, English-language training, and even gospel bracelets.

We have passed out hundreds of thousands of free gospel bracelets in India. These simple silicone wristbands show five colors (black, red, white, green, and yellow) and say *Jesus loves you*. They come with a small insert with Scriptures written in the local language. We ask people if they would like a bracelet that tells the story of Jesus. Then we explain the colors:

Black = sin

Red = blood of Jesus

White = forgiveness of sin

Green = growing in a living relationship with God

Yellow = eternal life in heaven (streets of gold)

Everyone wants a bracelet. We can be among Hindus, and they all want one. The same with Muslims. Everyone is so curious about generosity. Months later, we can go back into these areas and still see people wearing their bracelets. You might think, "So what? It's a cheap bracelet and there is no guarantee for salvation." But that's the point. Even inexpensive gospel bracelets become attractive to people far from God when distributed with audacious generosity. I have witnessed God use audacious generosity to transform thousands of people far from Him.

The Christian faith is the only movement in the world calling people to lay down their lives for their friends. No other world religion will ever top Jesus in audacious generosity.

When Believers come together in unity to demonstrate Christ in action through audacious generosity, the impact for the gospel is limitless. I have no doubt we can see the Great Commission fulfilled.

LIVE RECKLESSLY TO EXPERIENCE MORE

Living recklessly for God is important because it is walking in the truth that you are blessed and highly favored by the Lord Jesus Christ. God is with you. He is for you. You and I no longer need to be driven to take care of ourselves, our families, or our lives.

Reckless is the opposite of considerate. Living recklessly for God is surrendering your consideration of yourself. It is not being inconsiderate of others. Notice the phrase "for God." This is not careless and thoughtless for recklessness' sake. This is careless and thoughtless about having to protect, provide, and produce for yourself. We become reckless for God as we seek first the presence of God, His righteousness, and His kingdom while trusting that He will add in everything we need (Matthew 6:33).

Let's face it; seeking the presence of God FIRST does not come naturally to us. We seek a million and one other things we need first. When we are covered up in need, it will seem reckless to seek God's presence first and trust Him to add in everything we need. I find God really means business about these two words of instruction, "seek first." As we seek first His presence, God honors His Word and adds in everything we need. I can't encourage you enough to make it your total focus to seek God's presence first. Understand that's your primary job in life. God's job is to add in everything you need. Seeking God's presence will seem reckless, but God is faithful.

The word "reckless" comes from the old English word *receleas*, meaning "careless, thoughtless, heedless." If you have a reckless attitude, you aren't concerned about what happens to yourself or others who are affected by your actions. Here, reckless is the opposite of considerate.

Audacious generosity is going to feel absolutely reckless at times. When the Apostle Paul said in Philippians 2:3 that we are to consider the needs of others as more important than ourselves, he is asking us to live recklessly for God in regard to our own needs. It is much safer to feed my family than to start asking God to give me food that others might eat. In the natural realm, that felt like a reckless act of inconsideration to our family.

In one year, we went from a family needing food to sharing food with over five hundred families per month. We never missed a meal, and we witnessed countless miracles. Sometimes all we want is a meal, but the mission of God is so much bigger than our need for food. The mission of God requires miracles. Meals are safe. Miracles are reckless.

When my family needed food, I had a choice. I could either focus solely on the physical aspect of my family's need for food, or I could shift my focus to the spiritual needs of others. As I was praying, God's Word kept guiding me to seek Him, His righteousness, and His kingdom so that all these other things would be added to me. God is so confident of His faithfulness to us that He rarely wants to talk to us about our needs. It's like He's saying, "I've got you. How about others?"

When you're hungry, it is reckless to surrender your hunger to God and take on the mission of sharing hope with others who are hungry but don't have the hope you've found. As I saw it, I was just hungry, but at least I knew God was for me. What's worse is those who are hungry and don't know God is with them.

As I look back over my life, I see that a sense of living recklessly for God has afforded me the opportunity to experience more of Him than I ever thought possible. This is the result of setting God free. Living recklessly for God is not just reading the Gospels, but experiencing what the disciples experienced when they left everything and started following Jesus. It's not just reading the Book of Acts in the Bible, but it is allowing the acts of God to continue through your own living relationship with Him.

The first step toward audacious generosity is setting God free. This will seem reckless, but living recklessly for God allows you to experience more than you ever thought possible. We need to set God free because controlling God and living with audacious generosity for God don't mix. Let me encourage you with three truths as you take this step:

1. Setting God free happens by daily asking God for more.
2. This will require a lifetime of courage.
3. Fortunately, before we need courage, God has already instructed us to take courage.

It all starts with asking God for more.

CHAPTER 2

ASK GOD FOR MORE

I remember the day I regretted becoming a Christian.

When I was thirty-one years old, I was married with three kids. I had just invested three years of blood, sweat, and tears to start a new church when the leaders of this church voted to fire me as their pastor. I felt broken beyond repair. I didn't just want to quit; I wanted to die. The agony made me regret becoming a Christian. God seemed more like a careless boss than a trusted Father or Friend. I felt so confused.

I regretted becoming a Christian because my understanding of master, mission, strategy, and generosity were all messed up. I trusted Jesus for salvation and was baptized when I was ten years old. At that time, I thought I had done all I needed to do to be a Christian. I was a Christian, and Jesus was my Savior but not my Master.

In high school, I was a "Christian," yet I had no sense of mission in my life. It was like being in water that's not wet. I was miserable. During my senior year in high school, I attended a gospel meeting where I prayed, "God, if there is more of you than I realize, I want to know."

That's when everything began to change. Instead of going out and partying with my friends, I started staying home, sitting on my bed, and reading the Bible for hours. God gave me such a hunger for more. I couldn't stop reading, which was ironic since I never liked reading. I began experiencing a love and peace I'd never experienced before. God began impressing upon me that He had a plan for my life.

That year, God radically transformed my life from the inside out. I went from wanting to drop out of high school to one year later entering college in order to answer God's call into full-time ministry.

Fourteen years later, working as a pastor for that new church, I recognized Jesus as my Master. I was a Christian with a mission and strategy, but I mistakenly thought everything depended on what I could give. This resulted in me being an insecure workaholic for God.

The problem in all of this was that I was a Christian who didn't value or pursue the presence of God. I was misunderstanding my identity in Christ and the ultimate reason for my existence.

If only you knew how I had filled up prayer journals, wanting the peace and the power of God in my life. Unfortunately, I wasn't pursuing the presence of God in my life. I was a Christian for over twenty years before I understood the value of God's presence. All during this time, I had been begging God for more, but I wasn't willing to accept that God's greatest gift will always be more of His presence. The peace and power I wanted so badly was found in His presence.

THE VALUE OF GOD'S PRESENCE

Within a few months after I was fired for being an insecure workaholic, God took me to India and changed my life. I was a Christian minister of the gospel, but I had never seen the value of God's presence the way I did in India. I saw orphans without shoes and toothbrushes, but, if they knew Jesus, they exhibited real peace and joy. I saw whole church congregations without musical instruments except for tribal drums. They didn't have any bulletins or budgets, but you could clearly tell who knew Jesus because they were filled with so much joy.

On the plane ride back home, I drew two crosses in my journal. On one cross, I wrote all the good things I used to pursue in life (acceptance, security, significance, influence, impact, etc.). On the other cross, I wrote, "The presence of God." I committed before God that I would spend the rest of my life pursuing His presence first and foremost.

Once I committed to passionately pursue the presence of God, it brought me courage and freedom that has resulted in audacious generosity. I would have never guessed that asking God daily for more could have such a profound impact on my life.

LIVING RELATIONSHIP WITH GOD

Reporter Dan Wooding shared his story of the day Mother Teresa, standing in a festering slum, told him, "Your poverty is greater than ours."

> "The spiritual poverty of the Western World is much greater than the physical poverty of our people...You, in the West, have millions of people who suffer such terrible loneliness and emptiness. They feel unloved and unwanted. The Western people are not hungry in the physical sense. They are hungry in another way. The West knows they need something more than money. They don't know what it is. What they don't know they are missing, really, is a living relationship with God."

Mother Teresa won the Nobel Peace Prize for her care for

the poor in Calcutta, India. I love her phrase, "living relationship with God." It's much more than labeling yourself a Christian. A living relationship with God involves pursuing God's presence and experiencing God as He works in and through us to extend His presence on the earth.

I like how Pastor Steven Furtick of Elevation Church explains it, too: "Your proximity to the presence of Christ becomes your provision for the challenges that you face."

Hopefully, you can relate to pursuing the presence of God. I hope you pursue a living relationship with God. I encourage you to accept your need and opportunity to ask God for more every day. Everything changed once I started asking God daily for more.

WHAT DOES IT MEAN TO ASK GOD FOR MORE?

To ask is to request someone to do or give something. To ask God for more is to request God to do or give more. Asking God is not pressuring ourselves or others. Asking God for more is accepting and taking action on the truth that God is a fountain that never runs dry (Isaiah 58:11). God always wants more and has more for us than we ever thought possible.

In Lamentations 3:22-23 (NLT) the author writes, "The faithful love of the Lord never ends. His mercies never cease. Great is His faithfulness; His mercies begin afresh each morning." God will never say, "There is nothing more I could want for you."

Asking God for more is waking up tomorrow and taking action again to ask God for more. Then the next day, and the next. The average lifespan in the United States today is 28,470 days or seventy-eight years. That's 28,470 mornings of waking up to more of God's love and mercies. Let's say we are above average and live to be 110 years old. That would be 40,150 mornings. Even in that, God will still be larger than life.

God has always wanted more for you, and He is ready to give you more. The Bible says that God knew you even before you were born (Jeremiah 1:5). Even before you knew God, He already knew you by name. He already knew the number of hairs on your head. God already loved you before you received His love and started loving Him in return.

Before you wanted forgiveness for your sins, God already wanted a relationship with you so much that He sent Jesus to die in your place. Before you wake up and go into God's presence, He has already invited you to boldly come in Jesus' name (Ephesians 3:12). Before you begin to fear, God has already said "fear not" 365 times in Scripture—once for every day of the year. Before you are hungry, God has already planted and harvested seeds for your food

(Matthew 6:26). The fact that God has already provided in advance everything you need is evidence that He has always wanted more for you.

So how do we ask God for more?

After I was fired and went to India, we went through that period of financial hardship in which I prayed, "Father give us food that others might eat." While we witnessed miracles, we also had to make major adjustments to keep in step with God. One night I found myself praying in the middle of the night, "Come, Holy Spirit, come." At this point, God had given us the opportunity to share food with hundreds of families a week. I was confident I was doing what God had given me to do, but there was no paycheck. When we couldn't pay our bills, I turned our minivan back over to the bank. A year later, our mortgage was foreclosed, and we were evicted out of our home. A few weeks later, we had to buy back our earthly possessions because the bank had given them to a local charity (more on this story later).

Six weeks later, we were living with a family from our church. At times, there were seventeen of us living in a three-bedroom house. During the day, we were out delivering food to needy families. Every evening, we'd all come together for dinner, and then we'd set up mattresses under the dinner table where our kids would sleep. The next day, we'd do it all over again. It was a mix of gore and glory.

On one particular evening, I couldn't sleep. Around 3 a.m., I found myself alone in the driveway, just pacing back and forth praying, "Come, Holy Spirit, come." At this moment in my life, I was aware that as much as we needed a house to call home, what we really needed more than anything was the presence of God. We needed comfort that money couldn't buy. God had lovingly stripped away our need for income and financial stability. What we needed more than anything was a miracle.

I want you to hear this: As God was guiding me to pray, "Come, Holy Spirit, come," what I was agreeing to in my spirit was that I needed the Miracle Maker more than I needed a miracle. I desired the Way Maker, not just a way. As I cried, "Come, Holy Spirit, come" the anthem of my heart was, "All I need is you." It wasn't a lyric in some worship song. It was the honest cry of my heart.

I also want you to hear this: Left to my own ways, I would have never done this. God offered, and I took so much courage and freedom. I can take no credit. That night was a breakthrough moment in my life. God led me to stop needing and asking for miracles and start asking for His presence above all else.

I'll come back to this story later, but you should know that six weeks later, without any money in our hands, God moved us into the largest house we'd ever called home.

We lived there for seven years as God wrote His story of audacious generosity in our lives. Setting God free in my life began with asking God daily for more.

Perhaps this will show where God stops and where we tend to stop:

> Come, Holy Spirit, come. Come, Holy Spirit, come. Come, Holy Spirit, come. Come, Holy Spirit, come. Come, Holy Spirit, come. Come, Holy Spirit, come. Come, Holy Spirit, come. Come, Holy Spirit, come. Come, Holy Spirit, come. Come, Holy Spirit, come. Come, Holy Spirit, come. Come, Holy Spirit, come. Come, Holy Spirit, come. Come, Holy Spirit, come. Come, Holy Spirit, come.

Did you read each word, or did you jump ahead? Some may consider this silly exercise a waste of paper. Why repeat, "Come, Holy Spirit, come" fifteen times? It only takes one time—right? I'm confident that God's willingness to hear us pray, "Come, Holy Spirit, come" extends much longer than our willingness to pray it. We could pray it fifteen billion times and God would be like, "Now, we're just getting started."

I have to admit to you, at first the phrase, "Come, Holy Spirit, come" seemed odd to me. Obviously, the Holy Spirit has already come. I don't repeat this because I'm waiting on the Holy Spirit to come. I believe God leads us to this phrase because He always has more for us. The Holy Spirit offers us a practical opportunity to experience God today.

The Bible teaches that the Holy Spirit is our Comforter, our Counselor, and our Helper, among other practical expressions. Some say don't ask for help, claiming, "God helps those who help themselves." The truth is that's nowhere in the Bible. I am aware of my endless need for comfort, wise counsel, and help. I don't pray, "Come, Holy Spirit, come," to get the Holy Spirit to show up. I also don't disregard Jesus or the Father. God led me to pray, "Come, Holy Spirit, come" because the Holy Spirit is a gift from God. I am saying, "Holy Spirit, you are welcome here," "God, I need your presence," "God, I desire you more than anything."

Even now, years later, I can't stop praying, "Come, Holy Spirit, come." I don't mean that is all I pray, but I am saying it is the recurring prayer of my heart. We could pray it 365 days in a row and it still won't be enough. I've never entered a place in which it wasn't needed. I've prayed, "Come, Holy Spirit, come" in Hindu temples, on cramped airplanes, during funeral services, when passing automobile accidents, and in the midst of family conflicts—you name it. It's not about repeating the words over and over. It's about the posture of our heart.

WHAT GOD'S MORE IS AND IS NOT

If you think asking God for more is about more cars, houses, parking spaces, and followers on social media, then you're going to be frustrated—unless you're asking for these things FOR Him.

God's more is always more *of* Himself or more *for* Himself.

I hope you will allow this truth to bring you freedom. I understand it can seem disappointing at first. I've been so covered up in need before that more of God's presence was the last thing I thought I needed. I get it. When we're looking over a stack of bills, it seems obvious that what we need is more money. When our stomachs are growling from hunger, it seems obvious that what we need is more food. Let's be real. When we feel scared or alone, we crave a physical hug from a live person, not just a Bible verse.

To ask God for more is to ask for more of God.

Here are four things God's more is not:

1. God's more is not us bossing God around.
2. God's more is not about material entitlement.
3. God's more is not about giving in order to gain.
4. God's more is not about our faith being some force that guarantees prosperity.

Is it okay with you that the more God wants you to experience is more of Himself? I can understand if you were hoping to experience more success, influence, or respect. I did. We all do. Actually, life is full of a variety of mores we'd love to experience. God created every more known to man. Don't dare think God only offers more of Himself. He loves to give us desires and then fulfill those desires, but God's greatest gift will always be His presence.

Asking God for more is about asking for more *of* God or more *for* God. I had to allow God to redeem the word "more." It won't surprise me if you have ever considered the word "more" to be a bad word. I did. I suspect we all do. We are taught not to be ungrateful. We are taught not to be greedy. Let me share with you how I was told we can't be Christian and ask God for more:

During my senior year of high school when God called me into the ministry, it was right in the middle of the rise and fall of The PTL (Praise the Lord) Club led by Reverend Jim and Tammy Faye Bakker. What started out as a ministry of sharing the good news of Jesus Christ turned into an elaborate fundraising scheme in order to maintain the Bakker's lavish lifestyle all in the name of ministry. With tears in their eyes for the poor, they collected millions of dollars from well-meaning donors only to buy extravagant houses, multiple Rolls Royce cars, jet planes, and even air-conditioned dog houses.

They started building a Christian version of Disney World, which included a vacation timeshare that they illegally oversold. People were shocked when they couldn't book their week at the resort. The scandal went on to include sex, drugs, and lavished greed. It all happened within one hundred miles of where I grew up.

The first time I met my wife's father before we were married, he asked me if I was going to be a televangelist and make them all rich, too. That was seriously his idea of ministry. Everyone, even those outside the church, knew about this scandal. The world knew it as the laughingstock of Saturday Night Live.

I was entering the ministry in the midst of this toxic environment. It was common for every conversation about God, The Church, or Christianity to include jokes about Jim and Tammy Faye Bakker. To say there was harsh judgment and condemnation against the "Prosperity Gospel" is putting it lightly. The church's response was that we most definitely should NOT be asking God for more. I don't mean a subtle suggestion. I mean like a bold, "How dare you be a Christian and ask God for more?"

I agree that unless it comes straight from the mouth of God, we are wasting our time with "name it and claim it" Christianity. I remember thinking, *"So, I have received the gospel, but it is wrong to be prospered? If the gospel isn't prosperous, then why have it?"* I can't be around Jesus and He not prosper me. Being far from God and being raised to life in Christ is prosperity. If that's not prosperity, then I don't know what is. I refused to believe that the gospel isn't prosperous.

God wants to redeem the word "more." God wants us to start asking for more. Nobody wants you to have more than God. Accept that God's more is always more *of* Himself or more *for* Himself.

Wanting and having more is not selfish or sinful.

It is where we find our more and what we do with it that can be selfish or sinful.

The enemy is sneaky. He has taken the ugly sin of greed and attached the word "more" to it. He knows that if he can stop you from asking God for more, then he can kill your purpose. God wants to redeem the word "more." He wants it back. If you don't remember anything else I say, remember God wants you to have more.

Now let's learn all we can about God's more.

GOD'S MORE IS CONDITIONAL ON OUR INTENT

Let me share with you another important truth:

God's more starts and ends with God's intentions.

In John 6, we have the record of the Feeding of the Multitude. Scripture clearly states that Jesus already knew what He intended to do. We watch a miracle unfold as one little boy's lunch is used to feed over 15,000 people. It started and ended with God's intentions.

In John 6:5-6, we read, "Therefore Jesus, lifting up His eyes and seeing that a large crowd was coming to Him, said to Philip, 'Where are we to buy bread, so that these may eat?' This He was saying to test him, for He Himself knew what He was intending to do," (NASB).

In James 4, we are warned about having selfish intentions. Scripture actually states that we don't receive from God because our intentions are not pure. James 4:2-3 says, "Yet you don't have what you want because you don't ask God for it. And even when you ask, you don't get it because your motives are all wrong—you want only what will give you pleasure," (NLT).

I need you to get this truth down deep inside you:

God's more starts and ends with God's intentions.

By this I mean, God's more is always to fulfill His purposes for His glory.

> God's more is always conditional on our willingness to ask with a purity of intent.

The whole idea is to set apart God's more for His glory.

As children of God, His blessings like His presence, peace, and power *to us* are guaranteed. He can only bless us. Why did God trust me with huge quantities of food for needy families? He trusted me because I was willing to give it away for His purposes and for His glory.

Drumroll, please. Are you ready for God to reveal His master plan? God told Philip: You give them something to eat (Mark 6:37). God told Peter: Feed my sheep (John 21:17). I have come to the conclusion God is ultimately saying, "You can stop asking only for yourself." He is saying, "I've got you. What about others? You are mine. What about others? I've guaranteed with my own character that I'm going to feed you. What about others?"

James 4:2-3 is worth repeating: "Yet you don't have what you want because you don't ask God for it. And even when you ask, you don't get it because your motives are all wrong—you want only what will give you pleasure," (NLT).

Suppose you and I go to God saying, "Father, I need more money to buy groceries." We should not be shocked when God says, "Take part of what you have and share it with the single mom next door who doesn't know how her family will eat tonight." This kind of illogical instruction from God WILL always seem reckless. This will seem like a reckless inconsideration of your family's need for food. Even so, please just do it.

Setting God free and living recklessly for God is where you will begin to experience more from God than you ever thought possible. The Bible contains multiple stories of people who gave to others thinking it would jeopardize their survival only for God to use it to bring revival. Every person in the Bible who lived recklessly for God not only survived, but thrived. On the authority of God's Word, this will happen in your life too. God is faithful and will not fail you.

Will you allow God to give through you? Where are the people of God who are willing to pray in the following way? Father, give me salary so that others can have a salary. Give me Bibles so others can have a Bible. Give me houses so others can have houses.

God is waiting on those who will pray: "Father, let me build someone else a house. Let me buy someone else a car. Let me give away more than I live on so others might have eternal life. Let me distribute 100,000 Bibles to unreached souls without a Bible. Let me pay for someone else to go to college." God's more is conditional on our intent.

WHY IS ASKING GOD FOR MORE SO IMPORTANT?

Our first granddaughter was born in January 2020. This beautiful little girl has captivated our hearts like none other. From the moment she was born, she has not stopped wanting more. She wants more food, more sleep, more clean diapers, more food, more sleep, more clean diapers. She never stops wanting more. We would never judge her and tell her wanting more is sinful. Her heavenly Father created her to cry when she doesn't get more. I refuse to perceive her cry for more as bad.

Asking God for more is important because it honors God's plan and provision about where we find our help. Asking God for more reminds us that He is God and we are not. It's hard for us to ask for help and often it is challenging to admit that we are in need. Sometimes we even pressure ourselves to show God that we are good. We definitely don't want to come across as ungrateful for what we have already received. It can even be embarrassing to need more.

But God's ways are higher. Through Jesus, He has already done for us what we could not do for ourselves. He's looking for dependency, not self-sufficiency. He has so much more to give us than we could ever ask for or imagine. It focuses our dependence to be on Him, not ourselves or others.

Often when I take mission teams over to India, they are shocked by the visual reality of idol worship. There are idols of worship in their homes, shops, and fields. Idols are on the dash of the cars and even in the middle of the roads. These idols may be man-made figurines of an elephant god, a monkey god, or other various religious figures. The worshippers put flower garlands around the necks of the idols, burn candles and incense to them, and put food and drinks out in front of them.

Now before we judge those who worship idols made from human hands, Americans face an even bigger problem. At least the people of India are honest. You can clearly see when they are looking to something else instead of Jesus for their more. Most Americans, myself included, are not so obvious. We idolize our bodies, money, careers, houses, and friends. America is just as full of false idols; we just don't display them out in front of everyone. We flash our cars, big houses, and credit cards. If anything, we are worse off in that we live in denial. We can worship Jesus and a bunch of other idols and no one even has to know.

WHAT RESULTS FROM ASKING GOD FOR MORE?

Asking God for more will force you to set God free. As we experience more of God's presence, we start understanding His values, His motives, His desires, His plan, His will, and on and on. We can't keep asking God for more only to then put Him in a box. That won't work. You'll have no choice but to set God free. The day you stop asking God for more will be the day after you stopped setting God free. There isn't a Christian on the planet who doesn't need this daily tension and confrontation. This is the pathway to spiritual transformation. The presence of God is worth the adjustments we have to make to live in His presence.

The very purpose of our existence is to experience God. Even the demons know God, but they don't experience Him. The more of Him we experience, the more of Him we receive.

What results from asking God for more is finding our God-given mission. Did you find forgiveness of your sins? Good. There's more. Help others find forgiveness for their sins too. Have you received a peace that surpasses all understanding? Good. God has more, so take some for others.

Asking God for more results in having purpose and meaning in your life.

Did Mother Teresa have some connection with God that was only available to her? How about Billy Graham? John Wesley? Dietrich Bonhoeffer? George Müller? The answer is no. Every one of them experienced, received, and gave more than they ever thought possible. They experienced, received, and gave. They experienced, received, and gave.

The first step toward audacious generosity is setting God

free. Setting God free happens by daily asking God for more. I want to challenge you to make the theme of your every prayer to ask God for more.

This will require a lifetime of courage, which we'll discuss in the next chapter.

CHAPTER 3

WE NEED COURAGE

Have you ever realized a gift you didn't know you'd been given?

That's courage for me. When I started writing this book, I thought it was going to be a book about courage. The more I dove into it, the more I realized it has been courage that afforded me audacious generosity. God combines courage and freedom to give us a life of audacious generosity. This means audacious generosity is available to anyone.

I encourage you to see your own need for courage. A living relationship with God comes with the undeniable need for courage. Setting God free will require a lifetime of courage.

Our need for courage is important because it represents our need for God. Why doesn't God just automatically make us courageous? I've been a Christ-follower for over four decades, and my need for courage has increased, not decreased; it is what keeps me dependent on God.

The need for courage comes simply from the reality that God is God and we are not. Courage is a choice and an act of obedience. Courage results from yielding to the Holy Spirit.

HOLY SPIRIT = SPIRIT OF COURAGE

I believe Scripture leans more toward courage being a *who* instead of a *what*. In 2 Timothy 1:7 (NLT), the Apostle Paul told Timothy, "For God has not given us a spirit of fear and timidity, but of power, love, and self-discipline." If God has not given us a spirit of fear, then what spirit has He given us? I believe Paul is saying God has given us the Holy Spirit. He has given us a spirit of courage.

To encounter God is to encounter love. The Bible says God is love and that love is the evidence of having been with God (1 John 4:7-21). The same is true of courage. God is courageous, and courage is evidence of having been with God (2 Timothy 1:7). We are instructed to take courage over and over in Scripture. Courage isn't a once and for all provision from God. We have to continuously take more courage just like we have to continuously yield to the Holy Spirit (Galatians 5:16-25).

In Joshua 1:9, God told Joshua, "Have I not commanded

you? Be strong and courageous. Do not be frightened, and do not be dismayed, for the LORD your God is with you wherever you go," (NIV).

I love how Pastor John Piper, an American Reformed Baptist Pastor, asks and answers this question: "Can I as a twenty-first century Christian Gentile, not a Jewish person, and not living when it was written—not being Joshua—can I take a promise made to Joshua and apply it to myself? My answer is yes."

Let that sink in. Piper says, "The same words are used in Isaiah 41:10, 'Fear not, for I am with you; be not dismayed'—those two phrases, *don't fear* and *don't be dismayed, for I am with you*. It's broadened out in Isaiah 41:10."

Everything we witness about God through Jesus—His presence, peace, and power—is within us through the Holy Spirit. The same power that raised Jesus from the dead is within us.

In John 16:7 Jesus says, "But I tell you the truth, it is to your advantage that I go away; for if I do not go away, the Helper will not come to you; but if I go, I will send Him to you," (NASB). Think about this. Here is our long-awaited Messiah now explaining how He is going to go back to the Father. Everyone listening had to be thinking, "This is not good, we are just beginning to understand and now you're leaving us?"

Jesus knew He was God. He knew how He had humbled Himself to be a human like you and me. Fully God and fully man, the presence of God through the Son is now geographically confined to His skin. So He says, "It is to your advantage that I go away; for if I do not go away, the Helper will not come to you; but if I go, I will send Him to you."

WE NEED COURAGE

Every time we see God giving Himself to people in Scripture, we hear them being told not to be afraid. Fear is a natural response to any encounter with God. The greater our faith, the greater our need for courage. We will always need courage to enter God's presence, to hear and obey His voice, to surrender to His ways and mission.

We need the courage to accept the reality that God's ways are much higher than our ways. Often after we trust Jesus for salvation, we resist the promptings of God because we are scared and resist our need for courage. Before salvation, God primes the pump by giving us the courage to confess our sins and trust in Jesus alone for salvation. We are learning how to experience, receive, and give more than we ever thought possible. This order is intentional because this is the order God establishes for salvation. Before salvation, God allows us to experience Him; otherwise we'd never decide to receive Him.

The more we experience, the more we are willing to receive.

Think about a trip to Costco or Sam's Club. The more you experience their free samples, the more willing you are to buy their products and receive more. Many people have experienced God, but never received Him.

Our need for courage is endless...

We need courage to enter God's presence.

We need courage to offer God the same freedom He has given to us.

We need courage to believe God is who He says He is and will do what He says He will do.

We need courage to hear God speak.

We need courage to obey what God says.

We need courage to pray what God prays.

We need courage to let the Holy Spirit pray through us.

We need courage to surrender our life to God.

We need courage to rejoice in suffering.

We need courage to go where God goes.

We need courage to do what God does.

We need courage to submit to God's ways when they seem illogical to us.

We need courage to accept God's kingdom systems like we have to lose our life to gain it.

We need courage to trust God's authority over the natural world when we see so much evil, pain, and suffering.

In my own experience, God led me to:

1. Prioritize His presence above everything else in my life.
2. Trust my needs to Him in order to focus instead on others who need God's presence.
3. Shift my focus from receiving to giving.
4. Shift my dependency from what I can produce to what God can produce.
5. Open my hands to Him.
6. Commit in advance to use what He puts in my hands for His mission.

Each of these required God-sized courage. As you make these adjustments, you will need God-sized courage too. This is how you set God free in your life and open the door to His audacious generosity through you.

PRACTICAL BENEFITS

If you would have told me when I was seventeen years old that God wanted a personal, loving relationship with me, I probably would have freaked out and ran away in fear. When you're not living for God, it is incredibly intimidating to think about being known by Him. We all expect Him to know our sins already. At first, I didn't desire a personal relationship with God, but now I do. Part of what drew me to God was the practical benefits. It has been more than three decades since I prayed, "God, if there is more to you than I realize, then I really want to know." It was there that I started asking God for more.

This is why I always focus on the practical benefits of knowing God. Courage is practical. So are love, wisdom, peace, and power. There isn't a person on the planet who doesn't recognize the need for more courage, more love, more wisdom, more peace, and more power. All of us can relate. We can also quickly agree that we're already seeking those things. No one has to be convinced to seek peace. We all seek to love and be loved. There isn't a good parent on the planet who doesn't seek wisdom.

When I'm speaking to someone who is far from God, I think about how practical God is. Even nonbelievers recognize the need for courage. When we share with them that the Holy Spirit is the Spirit of Courage, we identify their need for courage and, ultimately, their need for a Savior. We also point them to God's provision. One of the most pivotal distinctions of the Christian faith over all world religions is God coming and dwelling within us through the Holy Spirit. We don't have an instruction manual to follow. We have the Helper within us.

THE CYCLE OF COURAGE

Before salvation, God starts a cycle of courage in all of our lives. Do you remember where you were when you accepted Christ? I was ten years old at an outdoor outreach program sitting on the bleachers by a high school football field. I remember during the invitation asking my father if I could go forward for prayer. My heart was pounding. My palms were sweating. God gave me courage. That night, I took Jesus only for salvation. I look back now and know that had God not given me courage, I don't know if I would have ever known Jesus.

How about you? When you trusted Christ, do you remember being fearful? If you went forward like I did, then it took courage to get up out of your seat and go forward to pray to trust Christ. Many have taken courage beside their beds or in a coffee shop with a trusted friend. The settings are endless. Each requires courage.

I've met so many Christians without a sense of mission. They have salvation for themselves, but they have no sense of mission in their lives from God. Does God only call some Believers and not others? No. As we read earlier in Matthew 28:18-20, Jesus gave us the Great Commission. This is not a mission for only some. A Believer without a mission is like water that's not wet. It's impossible. It can't be.

For example, look at Abraham. God told Abraham, "I will bless you and make you a blessing." Abraham is the spiritual father of every follower of Christ. We all know people who are dormant in their relationship with God because they took the blessing, but are yet to become a blessing. Why do some Believers become a blessing to others while others just stay blessed but never become a blessing to others? The difference is found in discovering the need for courage, our obedience to God, and whether we choose to be a blessing or not.

Courage is a choice. At salvation, we experience God, receive Jesus, and give our lives to God. The very next morning, the opportunity to experience, receive, and give continues. God always has more for us. The more of God we experience, the more courage we will need.

Let's not kid ourselves. Every one of us has experienced knock-down, drag-out fighting with God, ourselves, and others over the fears that rise up when we are confronted with how much higher God's ways are compared to ours. Oh, we need courage, alright.

Anyone who says following Christ is for wimps has clearly never met Jesus. Thank God He primes the pump with courage before salvation so we can make the choice to trust Jesus for salvation. If God didn't prime the pump with courage, we'd never know Jesus.

As I said, once we come to Jesus, courage becomes a choice. It is best seen in what I refer to as The Courage Cycle. Allow me to explain:

NEED COURAGE

Receive More of God

Take Courage

Ask God for More

As we ask God for more, we receive more of Him. The more of God we receive, the more courage we need to obey. So, we take more courage and ask God for more. The more courage we take, the more of God we receive. The more of God we receive, the more courage we need to take.

The first time God gave me courage to ask Him for more was when I prayed, "God, if there is more to you than this, then I want it." The more I experienced God, the more courage I needed. The more courage I took, the more of God I received. The more of Him I received, the more courage I needed in order to obey God. The more courage I took, the more of Him I received.

ACCEPT YOUR NEED FOR COURAGE

Will you acknowledge your need for courage? How can any of us encounter God and not need courage? If you are a born-again follower of Christ and don't need courage, then perhaps you have accepted only half of Abraham's blessings. You have allowed God to say, "I will bless you," but you refuse to allow Him to say, "and I will make you a blessing."

I can't help you set God free and have a life of audacious generosity if you're not willing to accept your need for courage. There is no way you can ask God for more and not need courage. If you don't need courage, ask yourself: do I really have an authentic relationship with God?

From the ages of ten to seventeen, I lived as a Christian without having a living relationship with Jesus Christ. At seventeen, I found myself miserable without any sense of mission for my life. When God said He had a plan for my life, He said, "I have blessed you, and now I will make you a blessing." I had to take courage to let God say, "Here is your mission."

Our part is to be an active participant of His strategy. God is on a mission to reveal Himself in the midst of human need. He has deposited Himself through the Holy Spirit into the life of every Believer. He is drawing all people to Himself. The Great Commission is a co-mission. It is Christ working in and through us to accomplish His mission. Audacious generosity is how God accomplishes the Great Commission. We, as Believers, are how God accomplishes this mission.

Audacious generosity has always been God's strategy. Has audacious generosity been your purpose? If we are going to experience this rich and generous God within us, then we are going to do it through audacious generosity. God offers no plan B. Focusing on our needs will only limit our experience.

Our purpose is to experience God. Freeing God is allowing God to be God. Freeing God is about not putting God in a box or compartmentalizing Him. It is about seeking God for who He is in His entirety. Freeing God is all about experiencing God. Freeing God allows us to experience more than we ever thought possible.

The first step toward audacious generosity is setting God free. Setting God free happens by daily asking God for more. This will require a lifetime of courage. The more of God we experience, the more courage we need to experience Him. Seeing our need for courage is critical, so we take the courage from God we need.

Before we need courage, however, God has already instructed us to take courage. Are you ready for some really good news?

CHAPTER 4

TAKE COURAGE

Don't you just love not having to wait for something you need? I know I do.

When it comes to courage, God has already made it available.

Did you know that nowhere in the Bible are we ever instructed to ask for courage? We are always instructed to take courage. See for yourself through the following verses: Deuteronomy 31:6-12, 2 Chronicles 32:5-8, Daniel 10: 17-19, Psalm 27:14, Psalm 31:24, Matthew 14:27, Mark 6:50, Mark 10:49, Matthew 9:2, Matthew 9:22, Acts 27:22, and Acts 27:25.

These are only a few verses instructing us to take courage. We don't even have to ask for courage. All we have to do is take it.

Now, that's easier said than done. No one should assume taking courage is automatic or easy. If it were, wouldn't all Christians be tithing, serving, and known for their audacious generosity? But don't be discouraged. While taking courage isn't automatic or easy, it is 100 percent possible. So how does someone take courage?

As with any transformation in our lives, half the battle is admitting our need for help. You'll never take courage if you never accept your need for it. You'll never need courage, for God's good reasons, until you start asking God for more. The good news is courage never runs out. Every time we need more courage, there is always more to take.

TAKING COURAGE = TAKING COURAGE

Courage is always available, but taking courage means taking courage. If you take a pen from someone, whose hand is it in? Your hand. If you take a book from someone, whose hand is it in? Your hand. If you take a cup of coffee from someone, whose hand is it in? Your hand. See how easy this is?

In the moments when we are frightened, God says, "You feel afraid, but the Holy Spirit is never afraid. Take courage. Yield to the Spirit. Let the courage of the Holy Spirit rise up within you." Despite your fear, you take courage as God has instructed you to. Now, whose hand is it in? Your hand. Just like that, you are now courageous.

I'm not talking about feelings. Courage is not a feeling. When Paul told Timothy, "God has not given us a spirit of fear," in essence, he was saying, "God has given us a Spirit of Courage" (2 Timothy 1:7). The opposite of fear is courage. The Holy Spirit is a courageous Spirit. Courage comes from a who.

It is okay to be weak. I want to say that again. It's okay to be weak. In 2 Corinthians 12:9-10, Paul shares how God told him, "My grace is all you need. My power works best in weakness. This is why I boast about my weaknesses so that the power of Christ can work through me. This is why I take pleasure in my weaknesses, and in the insults, hardships, persecutions, and troubles that I suffer for Christ. For when I am weak, then I am strong," (NLT).

Taking courage was one of the first transformations God made in my life, which is ironic to me, because I was a nervous wreck as a child and into early adulthood. I wet the bed until I was seven years old, which made me incredibly insecure. I was that nervous kid always wearing the "kick me" sign in school. I cowered to every school bully and if that wasn't bad enough, I remember countless times being flogged and chased by one of the roosters on our family's farm.

I used to get nervous about sweating, which then made me sweat even more. You should have been there the first time I ever preached. I was a seventeen-year-old sweating machine. I pinned absorbent liners to the inside of my suit coat in an attempt to absorb my nervousness. Still, that didn't work. I can't tell you the number of times I finished speaking only for the sweat rings under my arms to have met in the middle of my chest. But knowing that courage was available for the taking through God, I took it.

It is important for you to understand that courage is no respecter of persons. It is available to anyone who will take it. Looking back at my life, I've had to take courage often to keep in step with God. That same courage is available for you and everyone else who is willing to take it.

This is great news because it will take a lifetime of courage to set God free and experience more of God than you ever thought possible.

Let's revisit the cycle of courage I shared in the previous chapter:

God's invitation to take courage is an invitation to ask for more *of* God. When we take courage, we get more of God. The more of God we experience, the more courage we will need. It doesn't take courage to push God away. It takes courage to set God free. It takes courage to obey what God says, to pray what God prays, and to do what God does.

No matter where you are in the courage cycle, it begins with asking God for more. God's more is always more *of* Himself or more *for* Himself. When we ask God for more, what we receive is more of God. And the more of God we receive, the more courage we need to obey.

The moment we need courage, we are instructed to take courage.

To take courage is to take more of God. We cannot ask for more courage but not more of God. It will never happen. We cannot take courage but then put God in a box. It will not work. Courage isn't a fruit of the Holy Spirit, it is evidence of the Holy Spirit. You can't take more of God and not receive courage. You can't take courage and not receive more of God.

THE PURPOSE OF COURAGE

Why doesn't God just say, "I'm God. You're not. My ways are higher. You're going to be scared a lot. Suck it up, buttercup, and follow me." Have you ever been obedient and fearful at the same time? Why doesn't God just leave us fearful? What's the big deal about courage?

Remember that Paul told Timothy that God has not given us a Spirit of fear. Earlier I said the opposite of fear is courage, but this is not fully true. If I set you free from your fears, then what I have given you is freedom. The purpose of courage is freedom. Courage is the pathway to freedom. God's desire is not just to change our emotions, but to change our existence. We don't need God to force us to encounter Him while enslaved to our fear. We need freedom.

In 2 Corinthians 3:17, it says, "For the Lord is the Spirit, and wherever the Spirit of the Lord is, there is freedom," (NLT). Notice it doesn't say there is courage. While courage comes from God, the purpose of courage is freedom. The reason God instructs us over and over to take courage is that we need freedom.

The purpose of courage is freedom. The benefit of taking courage is freedom. It's not possible to be fearful and generous at the same time.

Courage results in freedom. Freedom results in audacious generosity.

HONOR THE PROCESS

I attended multiple leadership conferences with Dr. John Maxwell. I watched him go from an unknown local church pastor to a world-renowned speaker and author. He said, "Everyone wants to be where I am, but very few are willing to do what I did to get here." His implication was powerful. I had witnessed his process, not just his success, so I knew exactly what he was saying.

Long before John Maxwell was an authority on leadership, he was an unknown leadership junky. In addition to serving the churches he pastored, he tirelessly researched to learn all he could about leadership. He believed everything rises and falls on leadership years before he wrote his book about it. He used to carry boxes full of notes, some even on napkins, he had collected on leadership. He implemented a work ethic, love for people, and an unquenchable thirst for God.

I remember the day he prayed over Shelly and me while standing in the middle of a road on the campus of Southern Wesleyan University in South Carolina. It was a great honor. This was before he became recognized as an authority on leadership.

In the same way, long before I began to give with audacious generosity, God took me through a process of experiencing and receiving His courage and freedom. It was a life-changing process, but the point is that it was a process. This doesn't mean the process will take you as long as it took me. I didn't have anyone pointing out to me God's strategy of audacious generosity and His process of courage and freedom in order to get there.

The moment we start talking about audacious generosity, everyone wants some.

Given the choice, every one of us wants to be more generous, but fear holds us back.

Audacious generosity is the by-product of courage and freedom.

Courage results in freedom. Freedom results in audacious generosity.

LESSONS ON AUDACIOUS GENEROSITY

In Luke 16, Jesus tells a funny story about a shrewd manager who generously gives away his boss' wealth:

> Jesus told this story to His disciples: "There was a certain rich man who had a manager handling his affairs. One day a report came that the manager was wasting his employer's money. So the employer called him in and said, 'What's this I hear about you? Get your report in order, because you are going to be fired.

The manager thought to himself, *'Now what? My boss has fired me. I don't have the strength to dig ditches, and I'm too proud to beg. Ah, I know how to ensure that I'll have plenty of friends who will give me a home when I am fired.'*

So he invited each person who owed money to his employer to come and discuss the situation. He asked the first one, 'How much do you owe him?' The man replied, 'I owe him 800 gallons of olive oil.' So the manager told him, 'Take the bill and quickly change it to 400 gallons.'

'And how much do you owe my employer?' he asked the next man. 'I owe him 1,000 bushels of wheat,' was the reply. 'Here,' the manager said, 'take the bill and change it to 800 bushels.'"

The rich man had to admire the dishonest rascal for being so shrewd and it is true that the children of this world are more shrewd in dealing with the world around them than are the children of the light. Here's the lesson: Use your worldly resources to benefit others and make friends. Then, when your possessions are gone, they will welcome you to an eternal home.

"If you are faithful in little things, you will be faithful in large ones. But if you are dishonest in little things, you won't be honest with greater responsibilities. And if you are untrustworthy about worldly wealth, who will trust you with the true riches of heaven? And if you are not faithful with other people's things, why should you be trusted with things of your own?" (Luke 16:1-12) (NLT)

Talk about courage. But also notice the freedom he was given. Every one of us would have the time of our lives giving away someone else's resources. If fear was removed and you had the freedom to give away someone else's resources, you would have the best life ever. That's audacious generosity.

LET GOD DEFINE GENEROSITY

To the world, generosity is to pay it forward. To the world, audacious generosity is giving to a cause. To God, generosity is one of His characteristics. For God so loved that He gave (John 3:16). So while we are at it, let's take back the definition of generosity. In today's culture, we celebrate only the generosity of the rich and famous. We define generosity primarily as giving money to a cause, but that is not the way God defines generosity.

For example, in Luke 21, Luke tells us about The Widow's Offering: "While Jesus was in the Temple, He watched the rich people dropping their gifts in the collection box. Then a poor widow came by and dropped in two small coins. "I tell you the truth," Jesus said, "this poor widow has given more than all the rest of them. For they have given a tiny part of their surplus, but she, poor as she is, has given everything she has," (NLT).

The lesson we see is that the widow loved God so much that she gave Him absolutely everything. Notice that Jesus said the rich people gave a tiny part of "*their* surplus." There are two issues here: 1) our view of what's ours (nothing) and what's God's (everything); 2) Giving what we can produce (tiny) versus giving what God can produce (limitless).

Audacious generosity happens when the dividers are removed from what is mine and what belongs to God. It is all God's. Audacious generosity is loving God enough to allow Him to use your hands, feet, and resources on earth the same way He used Jesus. Through Jesus, God has given us everything. Audacious generosity is giving everything back to God just like this widow.

God's definition of audacious generosity is loving Him enough to give back absolutely everything He has given to you.

THE PURPOSE OF FREEDOM

We just agreed that God's purpose of courage is freedom, so what is the purpose of freedom? We find the answer in Galatians 5:1. Paul writes, "It is for freedom that Christ has set us free," (NIV).

I know what it is like to not experience freedom. I know what it is like to be paralyzed by fear, guilt, and rejection.

Earlier I shared with you how I was fired by the church I had planted. Unfortunately, the baggage of my childhood had resulted in a performance-based relationship with God. No attendance, offering, or success was ever enough. I thought my life's purpose was to do great things for God.

Growing up, when my father would get angry at me, he would yell, "Kevin, you'll never amount to anything!" That message played over and over in my head. I was a Christian ministry leader in bondage to the fear of failure, and I drove the new leaders of this new church crazy—to the point they released me as their pastor.

It was the most painful experience in my life. At the time, I felt so betrayed by God. "This is not how it is supposed to turn out," I thought to myself. "Is this what I get for answering the call to the ministry?" I didn't want to just quit; I wanted to die. I felt so ashamed.

Thankfully, God sent some brothers of Christ into my life who discipled me in my identity in Christ. My friends took me through an exercise of applying biblical forgiveness. It was thorough. I began to see that when God forgives us, He agrees to live with the consequences, agrees to not seek revenge, and He chooses to forgive.

My friends walked me through an exercise of praying for the Holy Spirit to bring to mind everyone who had ever caused me to feel fear, guilt, or rejection. I wrote down about forty names, mostly those who had worked to have me fired. Forgiving my dad, myself, and releasing false expectations I had held against God were the most difficult and impactful. Obviously, God doesn't sin against us. Technically we can't forgive Him, but we can free Him from false expectations and wedges between us.

I also grieved for all the pain my insecurities had caused so many people. It was there that I experienced freedom in Christ. For the first time in my life, my security, acceptance, and significance depended on Christ and not myself.

I remember thinking, "Wow. This is what it is like to be free? You mean I never have to preach again, tithe, or even lead another person to Christ and God loves me just the same?" In my mind, the ministry went from a "have to" to a "get to." I get to preach again. I get to tithe again. I get to lead yet another person to Christ.

The purpose of freedom is freeing God, ourselves, and others.

Most people love the verse: You will know the truth and the truth will set you _____ (John 8:32). We all love the verse: who the son sets _____ is _____ indeed (John 8:36). See you know it. One of the verses the enemy gets most of us to miss is the verse: it is for ____ that Christ has set us ____ (Galatians 5:1). Think about this verse. If we are free then who else needs to be freed? If you are alive in Christ then you are free indeed, so who else needs to be freed? It is for freedom that Christ has set us free. Who else needs to be freed?

Have you offered God the same freedom He has offered you? Most people don't even realize they can ask that question. The Bible says we love because He first loved us (1 John 4:19). We respond in freedom in response to the freedom He has given us just like we love because He loves us. In the same way, the Bible says we give because He gave to us (John 3:16). Let us hear Him proclaim, "I've freed you so that you will free me."

Is God free to be who He says He is and do what He says He will do?

As I see it, we have two choices: We can keep God in a box in an attempt to maintain control, or we can take courage and set God free. God is not enslaved to us. God is not tied up. Free God to do what He wants to do in and through you. Offer God the same freedom He has given to you.

Remember the courage cycle I shared earlier? The moment you stop taking courage, you stop asking for more of God.

The moment you stop asking for more of God, you no longer need courage. Can you see yourself in the courage cycle? If not, will you take courage to live recklessly by giving God the freedom He has given you? Trust me. The more freedom you offer God, the more courage you're going to need. In fact, you will need a lifetime of courage.

The more freedom in Christ I experience in me, the more audacious generosity I experience through me. You will never be completely free until you set God free. The very reason for courage is so that we will set God free.

Here comes my favorite part of the section. Time to apply God's Word.

CHAPTER 5

APPLICATION

SET GOD FREE—LIVE RECKLESSLY TO EXPERIENCE MORE

The first step toward audacious generosity is setting God free. We just spent the last three chapters discussing the following:

1. Setting God free happens by daily asking God for more.
2. This will require a lifetime of courage.
3. Fortunately, before we need courage, God has already provided courage and instructed us to take courage.

Now, let me walk you through three practical applications you can make in order to set God free in your life:

APPLICATION #1: COMMIT TO PASSIONATELY PURSUE THE PRESENCE OF GOD

Take out your journal and then draw two crosses so you can write inside them. Pray and ask the Holy Spirit to reveal to you things that you seek. In the first cross, make a list of what comes to mind. I wrote "acceptance, security, significance, influence, and impact." Consider these and add your own. Do you ever seek what you can get from God instead of God Himself, or the presence of God? Let your list be as long as you need. Once you're done, I want you to write, "The Presence of God" on the other cross. Take time and meditate on Matthew 6:33. Pray and commit to God to passionately pursue His presence above all else.

To help me, I set a reminder on my phone that pops up every morning with the word, "presence," reminding me to pursue the presence of God. I encourage you to do whatever you need to remember and honor your commitment. Decide now that you will prioritize and make time for the presence of God every day. I encourage you to integrate, "Come, Holy Spirit, come" into every prayer you say. Agree with God that His greatest gift is the gift of His presence. Commit to asking Him for more every day. Agree with God that nothing is greater than His presence.

Key Verse: Seek the Kingdom of God above all else and live righteously, and He will give you everything you need (Matthew 6:33 NLT).

The Point: We set God free when we passionately pursue His presence.

APPLICATION #2: COMMIT TO ASK FOR THE HOLY SPIRIT'S HELP

Ask God for greater awareness of the Holy Spirit. Take time to meditate on John 16:13 and John 14. Jesus offers very practical insight into the benefits of the Holy Spirit in our everyday lives. The Holy Spirit is a Helper we should depend on every day. A modern analogy of a helper is a coach. Let the Holy Spirit be your inward Coach in how to study God's Word, pray, give, respond to conflict, and even find your phone when you lose it. He's that practical and personal. Ask for the Holy Spirit to guide you when you are reading the Word. Nothing energizes our study of God's Word more than pulling our chair up in front of the Holy Spirit. Let Him show you where to start, what He is saying to you, and how to apply it to your life today. Let the Holy Spirit pray through you. You can always be confident of the Holy Spirit praying according to the will of God. The Holy Spirit's prayers will always be answered. This is what Paul is talking about in Ephesians 6:18, when he says, "Pray in the Spirit on all occasions with all kinds of prayers and requests. With this in mind, be alert and always keep on praying for all the Lord's people," (NIV).

I want you to admit your need for courage. Until you come

to a place of needing courage, you can't begin to take courage. You're not going to go after something you don't think you need. Take your journal and write out a prayer asking God for the Holy Spirit's help. If you don't already, I encourage you to commit to know the Holy Spirit equally to the Father and the Son. God used the book, *God Guides*, by Mary Geegh to teach me the practice of listening prayer. I highly recommend reading the book. When our kids were small, we used *God Guides* in our family devotions. Nothing fosters a living relationship with God more than hearing Him speak.

Key Verse: When the Spirit of truth comes, He will guide you into all truth. He will not speak on His own but will tell you what He has heard. He will tell you about the future (John 16:13) (NLT).

The Point: We set God free when we accept the help of the Holy Spirit.

APPLICATION #3: SURRENDER YOUR FEARS ABOUT GOD

Acknowledge what scares you about God. In your journal, prayerfully answer these questions:

- What scares you about doing what God says to do?
- What scares you about going where God says to go?

- What scares you about letting God pray through you?
- What scares you about having to adjust your life to God's values?

You should have a list of specific fears. If you haven't already, I want you to add "the fear of embarrassment" and "the fear of disappointment" to your list. When it comes to the fear of embarrassment, so often we miss out on experiencing more of God worrying about what other people will think. When it comes to the fear of disappointment, I want you to deal with the fact that sooner or later, God will absolutely disappoint you. Yep. I just said that. What will you do when God doesn't make sense? Are you going to divorce God? Unfollow God? No. Like Job, you will take courage and say, "Though God disappoints me, yet I will put my trust in God" (Job 13). The truth is God is God and you are not. It is okay for God to be scary. The Bible is full of examples of people who needed courage as they encountered God. You are not the first. You will not be the last. I want you to admit your fear of the unknown. Our God who knows everything already knows the future. We don't. In fact, so much is unknown to us. Every one of us fears the unknown. In your journal, write out a prayer surrendering your fears about God.

Key Verse: So if you sinful people know how to give good gifts to your children, how much more will your heavenly Father give good gifts to those who ask Him. (Matthew 7:11) (NTL).

The Point: We set God free when we face our fears about God.

CONGRATULATIONS ON SETTING GOD FREE

The result of setting God free is that it allows you to experience more of God than you ever thought possible. This is freedom like you've never imagined it before. I remember the day God began to connect my freedom with His freedom. It was at that moment I realized God had set me free so that in return, I could set Him free.

Setting God free will seem reckless at times. That's okay. Living recklessly for God is what will allow you to experience more of God than you ever thought possible.

Commit to taking this journey of audacious generosity. Every single act of audacious generosity I face requires me to offer God more freedom. I didn't just set God free twenty years ago. Every single occurrence of audacious generosity comes with the pounding conviction from our Heavenly Father saying, "I want you to set me free. I want you to believe I am who I say I am. I want you to experience me for who I really am. I want to use this to draw people to myself. Set me free." I encourage you to keep allowing God to say, "Just set me free." When we set God free, we are one step closer to audacious generosity.

Audacious generosity is where God is the Giver, and giving depends on what God gives through you. Audacious generosity happens in the context of a living and growing relationship with God. It begins when we stop depending on what we can produce and start depending on what God gives through us. The result of God giving through us is us then experiencing the miraculous proportions only God can produce. This is where giving becomes fun. This is how we find meaning and impact in our lives. Audacious generosity is a movement where Believers around the world unite to fulfill the Great Commission.

The second step toward audacious generosity is setting yourself free, which we'll dive into next.

SECTION 2

SET YOURSELF FREE

CHAPTER 6

LIVE EXPECTANTLY TO RECEIVE MORE

Respecting the power of expectations in the natural realm is important.

In 1962, Japanese scientists conducted an experiment. They told thirteen boys they were touching their arm with a nonpoisonous leaf but used a poisonous leaf instead. Only two of the boys showed any skin reaction. Then, they told the boys they were touching their other arm with a poisonous leaf but used a nonpoisonous leaf instead. All thirteen boys showed a skin reaction that was greater than the reaction from the exposure to the poisonous leaf. According to this study, the mere expectation of being touched with a poisonous leaf can bring on a skin eruption.

Expectations matter.

THE POWER OF EXPECTATIONS

Respecting the power of expectation in the spiritual realm is even more important.

The power of expectations doesn't just apply to medicine, sickness, and healing. It has a powerful impact on our faith and relationship with God. One of the most bizarre scenes in the Bible is recorded in Matthew 21:1-11. We refer to it as the story of Palm Sunday:

> "As they approached Jerusalem and came to Bethphage on the Mount of Olives, Jesus sent two disciples, saying to them, 'Go to the village ahead of you, and at once you will find a donkey tied there, with her colt by her. Untie them and bring them to me. If anyone says anything to you, say that the Lord needs them, and He will send them right away.' This took place to fulfill what was spoken through the prophet: 'Say to Daughter Zion, See, your king comes to you, gentle and riding on a donkey, and on a colt, the foal of a donkey.' The disciples went and did as Jesus had instructed them. They brought the donkey and the colt and placed their cloaks on them for Jesus to sit on. A very large crowd spread their cloaks on the road, while others cut branches from the trees and spread them on the road. The crowds that went ahead of him and those who followed shouted, 'Hosanna to the Son of David! Blessed is

He who comes in the name of the Lord. Hosanna in the highest heaven.' When Jesus entered Jerusalem, the whole city was stirred and asked, 'Who is this?' The crowds answered, 'This is Jesus, the prophet from Nazareth in Galilee,'" (NIV).

Our expectations are powerful. The Bible records this as Jesus' triumphal entry into Jerusalem before He is crucified. Jesus went to Jerusalem to be beaten beyond recognition and hung on a cross for our sins, so wouldn't you expect this to be more of a funeral procession? Instead, it's a huge celebration.

Notice that we are told the whole city of Jerusalem was stirred up. A large crowd gathers. Often we focus on the display of Jesus' humility. We also see praise and worship. Some are taking their coats off or cutting palm branches and laying them on the road in front of Jesus. Notice how everyone is shouting praise to God. This isn't a funeral procession. This is a party. It's a worship celebration. Everyone is overflowing with joy.

THE PARTY BEFORE THE CROSS

Who in their right mind throws a party before the cross? God does.

Even today, Christians celebrate Palm Sunday, and it is always a joyous occasion of blessing leading into what we call Passion Week or Holy Week. The following Friday is called Good Friday. We remember how Jesus was arrested, put on trial, beaten beyond recognition, and shamefully crucified on the cross. He died an agonizing death before being laid in the tomb. The crucifixion of Christ is one of the most gruesome events in world history.

In Mathew 21, the crowd was not even aware of the crucifixion as we are now. They were simply celebrating that they knew Jesus. They likely expected Jesus to assume His role as their earthly king, but instead, a crucifixion happened. If only they knew to be expecting a funeral. A few days later, they would agree with Jesus being crucified. We know that God was ordaining these events to accomplish our salvation.

So why did God throw a party on Palm Sunday? The answer comes down to expectation. God expected the cross to result in reconciling the world back to Him. This was the whole reason the Father had sent the Son. Since the rebellion of Adam and Eve, mankind had a problem called sin. God had a plan named Jesus. That day the people had no idea Jesus would be crucified on a cross just five days later. God did! God knew three days later Jesus would rise from the dead, proving He alone held the keys to eternal life. Palm Sunday is God celebrating in advance.

God throwing a party before the cross comes down to

expectation. This is a prime example of how God's ways are higher than ours. Can you imagine the cities of two NFL teams throwing victory celebrations the week before the Super Bowl? That would never happen. They have to wait to see the outcome of the game before they can celebrate. We celebrate in response. God celebrates in advance. Why? Because God knows how the story ends.

In the book of Hebrews, we see how Jesus knew the ending of the story. Look at this passage from Hebrews 12:2 (NIV): "For the joy set before Him Jesus endured the cross, scorning its shame, and sat down at the right hand of the throne of God." Notice the language: "For the joy set before Him." You can have a celebration without joy, but you can't have joy without a celebration. This is powerful and applies right where life gets real for us.

CELEBRATING IN ADVANCE

What if we started celebrating in advance? Is it even possible? Yes, it is. It is not only possible, it is expected.

Look at Philippians 4:6 (NIV), "Do not be anxious about anything, but in every situation, by prayer and petition, with thanksgiving, present your requests to God." Did you catch the phrase "with thanksgiving?" Thankful for what? Just as we can be thankful for what God has done, we can also be thankful in advance for what He will do.

Faith is not celebrating in response to what has already happened. That doesn't require faith. You and I are called to be people of faith. We are following a God who celebrates in advance. We also know how this story ends. It takes faith to celebrate in advance. As a parent, I don't want my kids to act surprised when I care for them as if they had doubts. I want them to be confident about how I will care for them. It honors God when we are thankful in advance for what He will do.

So, why do we insist upon waiting to celebrate in response?

We may think, "If God saves my friend, then I will celebrate. If God heals my cancer, then I will celebrate. When God provides for my college, then I will celebrate." Can you hear the lack of faith? *If* God. *If* God. *When* God. No more. Stop. God celebrates in advance. Even when we aren't confident in God's character, He is confident in His character. He knows His promises. He knows how the story ends, and so should we.

When I look back on my life, I realize that I endured unnecessary trauma by hosting endless boxing matches with God. My expectations of God were in response to what He did or didn't do. I was always trying to prove His love for me. If He gave me success, then I would know He loved me. If He bailed me out financially, then I would know He loved me. If I received an unexpected blessing, then I'd know He loved me.

One day I realized that if the cross didn't prove His love for me, then nothing would. I began to understand that He had already proven His love for me in advance. I began to be confident of His love for me even if He never did anything else for me. There were no more "ifs" or "whens." God didn't owe me anything. I owed Him everything. This pivot changed my relationship with God, and those internal boxing matches were over.

It is incredibly insulting to the Creator and Savior of the world when we act so insecure.

Say your mom is in the kitchen preparing a nice dinner for you and your relatives. One by one, you and your relatives enter and start questioning what she is doing. You all start questioning whether your mom even cares. You and your relatives show no appreciation to your mom for preparing dinner. Rather, your mom hears everyone's uncertainty, insecurity, and sense of insignificance. This will break her heart. She may think, "Why is everyone communicating this lack of trust? "Why are they acting as if they are so unloved?" It would be a total contradiction to her character and care for you and your relatives.

I hope you've never done this to God. Unfortunately, I have many times. It's different today, though. I'm learning to celebrate in advance, and you can too. It boils down to expectations. Is there ever a time we should wait to celebrate the faithfulness of God? The only answer is no.

So often, we pray for a breakthrough in a particular area. Celebrating in advance *is* the breakthrough.

God knows the ending, so He celebrated in advance the results of the cross. Even knowing the pain, He celebrated the victory. We can allow this principle to fuel our faith and obedience. There's no need to wait until we see the answers to our prayers to celebrate the favor and blessings of God. We know the ending. He's worthy now, not when He does one more thing for us. Celebrate in advance.

All the enemy can do is pervert the truth. He knows the ending too. He knows God is faithful, so the enemy lies and tricks us to wait until God's provision to celebrate. We live in fear and anxiety instead of confident hope. The difference is huge. Anxiety and fear produce bondage, which causes us to avoid God. Confident hope produces thanksgiving, which fuels our worship of God. In the context of audacious generosity, our expectations either hold back our generosity or they fuel it.

Do you celebrate in expectation?

THE IMPACT OF EXPECTATIONS ON AUDACIOUS GENEROSITY

In John 6:1-14 when Jesus fed the multitude, how much did the disciples hold in their hands? Before they found a little boy's lunch box, the disciples had nothing in their hands. God isn't waiting for your hands to be full before you can start giving. If you commit to give even with empty hands, God can fill your hands.

That is exactly what happened in the miracle of the Feeding of the Multitude. The disciples had nothing. They found a little boy with some fish and loaves. They brought the food to Jesus, which had to take a lot of courage. It was tiny compared to the need, but it was all they could produce. Jesus then said, "Have all the people sit down." He broke the fish and loaves, blessed them, and gave them to the disciples to distribute. It had to take even more courage to start distributing the fish and loaves to the people, knowing that it wasn't enough. But then something miraculous happened: the multiplication took place in the disciples' hands.

The same hands that earlier held nothing were now the hands being used to give. When it comes to audacious generosity, the Creator of the universe who made all we see out of nothing, does not require anything from you in order for you to give; He only requires your obedience. You need nothing in your hands in order for God to give through you. Audacious generosity depends upon the measure God can produce (limitless), not on the measure you can produce (tiny). The only thing God needs from you is your open hands.

STEP #2: SET YOURSELF FREE

Have you ever witnessed miracles like the Feeding of the Multitude with your own eyes? I have. Have you ever watched multiplication occur in your own hands like we see in the miracle of the Feeding of the Multitude? I have. You, too, can witness a lifetime of miracles like the Feeding of the Multitude. To do so requires you to let God change your expectations. God combines courage and freedom to change our expectations.

Unfortunately, we as Believers often don't do ourselves any favors by fighting in three boxing matches. These boxing matches keep us from audacious generosity:

1. The first boxing match is fear versus freedom.
2. The second boxing match is working versus resting.
3. The third boxing match is reprimand versus reward.

As we consider each boxing match in the following chapters, determine which side is winning in your life. The side that's winning indicates what you expect from God. What you expect determines whether you celebrate in response or in advance. What you expect determines whether your hands are opened or closed.

Do you live expectantly from God? If the answer is no, then at the end of this section, my hope is that your answer will be yes.

In section one, we saw how vital it was for us to set God free as the first step toward audacious generosity. The second step toward audacious generosity is setting yourself free. Living expectantly from God allows you to receive more than you ever thought possible. We need to set ourselves free because expectations matter and impact audacious generosity.

In the next chapter, we'll tackle how to end the boxing match between fear and freedom.

CHAPTER 7

FEAR VERSUS FREEDOM

Fear is a B-word—a bully. Maybe you thought I was going to use a different B-word. Both are true.

The first boxing match we face is between fear versus freedom. Do you find yourself responding to the challenges of life out of fear or freedom? At some point in all our lives, everyone feels bullied by fear. I'm fully convinced, however, that God wants us to respond to the challenges of life out of freedom. I didn't always think this way, though. For the longest time, I responded out of fear. I used to be incredibly insecure, but now my security is in Christ.

Let today be the day this boxing match comes to an end for you.

The majority of psychologists say the number one fear is

death. The fear of death is what fuels the fear of spiders, public speaking, and heights. I don't think it was any coincidence that at just seventeen years old, the very first sermon I ever preached was based on 2 Timothy 1:7 (NLT): "For God has not given us a spirit of fear and timidity, but of power, love, and self-discipline." God has used this verse to guide me throughout my life and I believe it's key to living expectantly from Him.

The Bible teaches us about physical death and spiritual death. At birth, we are all born physically alive, but spiritually dead. If nothing changes, the only thing we have to fear is physical death because we are already spiritually dead. This boxing match between fear and freedom will go on until we expect the Holy Spirit to fill us with the power, love, and self-discipline we read about in 2 Timothy 1:7.

PERFECT LOVE CASTS OUT FEAR

Before Christ, we're all born with a spirit of fear, but when we are born again through faith in Jesus Christ, we receive a different spirit. The Holy Spirit now lives within us. Eternal life isn't a certificate or slip of paper but is found in the person of Jesus Christ. The presence, power, and peace of the Lord Jesus Christ has been deposited into you through the Holy Spirit. When you are afraid, He is not. Scripture tells us that perfect love casts out fear. My friend, fear is gone.

I lived in fear for twenty years after I accepted Jesus for salvation. It wasn't until I was thirty years old that I began to understand what the Bible says about our identity in Christ. Before Christ, we are all born in fear, guilt, and rejection. Once we are alive in Christ, we are secure, significant, and accepted in Christ.

When I was ten years old, I knew the fear of uncertainty about what happens when we die. I knew I didn't want to spend eternity in hell, so I accepted and believed in Jesus only for salvation. I got my "fire insurance." At that moment, I was physically and spiritually alive. For me, the problem was that I never understood my salvation was a work of God, which could never be undone. I was taught to fear that I could lose my salvation.

It wasn't until I found freedom in Christ when I was thirty years old that I began to see for myself that, according to the Bible, we are either eternally secure or we are eternally insecure. All of a sudden, the boxing match between fear and freedom ended. My expectations had shifted, and I no longer expected death. I understood that I couldn't undo God's forgiveness. I also began to see that to be absent from the body is to be present with the Lord. In Christ, we have been made secure, significant, and accepted. I was free no matter what happened to me. I now expected freedom.

If you struggle to be characterized by fear rather than freedom, then I highly recommend Dr. Neil Anderson's *Finding Freedom in Christ* study. It helped me understand that harboring bitterness from unforgiveness was holding me back from experiencing God's gift of freedom in Christ. As we continue, we'll see more about the connection between our forgiveness and God's gift of freedom through Christ.

When you begin filtering your views and decisions through freedom instead of fear, you'll begin to see just how fearful the world is. You'll see just how fearful you've been. Fear is profound and widespread. Most major news channels use fear to sell their news, and we take it hook, line, and sinker.

Allowing God to set me free enabled me to offer God the same freedom in return. As I set God free, He began to confront me on my need to set myself free. I found myself needing to take courage to offer myself the same freedom God had given me. When I did, God gave me a whole new set of expectations—the first of which was freedom.

In Romans 6, 7, and 8, Paul identifies this boxing match. It's the battle between our old self and the new self—the old mindset and the new mindset. The conflict is not because we are waiting for God to set us free, but because we haven't yet set ourselves free. We haven't yet traded the expectation of fear for the expectation of freedom. His freedom has been provided, but if we don't expect it, then we can miss out on experiencing freedom.

If you look at Paul's discourse in Romans 6, 7, and 8, he shows that Jesus comes and declares freedom to be the winner of this boxing match. Unfortunately, we often continue to live in the same mindset of fear we've always known. This is why Paul told the Romans, "Do not conform to the pattern of this world, but be transformed by the renewing of your mind" (Romans 12:2) (NIV).

I lived contrary to the truth of freedom in Christ for the first twenty years of my Christian life and gospel ministry. How does this happen? If God has set us free, then how does this boxing match continue? It takes a dedicated decision to accept the new mindset of freedom. Freedom doesn't come natural to us like fear does. Freedom is a right to every Believer. The victory of this boxing match has shifted from fear to freedom. Freedom in Christ is as much a reality as the law of gravity. It doesn't matter what you think or feel. You are free, so you should expect freedom. The boxing match is over.

Ending the boxing match between fear and freedom is extremely important. Fear impacts our prayers, praise, and worship. Often the issue of the spiritual war going on inside us is the difference between fear and freedom. Worship is one of our weapons. If the enemy can succeed in halting our worship, then he can steal, kill, and destroy our sense of freedom (John 10:10). He can traumatize our emotions. He can erode our confidence. He can steal our joy. We don't have to sit in fear waiting for disaster. We can sit in faith knowing that freedom is our inheritance and identity.

Let me make one thing clear: we are not waiting on God to set us free. If you are alive in Christ, then you have been set free from the bondage of fear. Experiencing fear temporarily and being controlled by fear are two different things. We can't control what makes us fearful, but we can control whether or not fear sticks to us. If fear is more than a temporary emotional response, then something is out of order. Because of Christ, freedom now trumps every occurrence of fear in our lives. Freedom is what sticks. Freedom is what shapes us. Freedom is what we can expect.

Is anything holding you back? Drugs, alcohol, addictions, finances, relationships? God has provided everything you need to overcome anything. Freedom is God's present provision, not a future hope. It seems some Christians are waiting to go to heaven in order to be set free. Scripture makes it clear that the ultimate freedom is freedom from sin. John 8:31-36 and Galatians 1:4 indicate that Jesus has set us free now in this life. Nowhere in Scripture are we told we have to wait to be set free. We have already been set free at the cross.

This is where the challenge begins. Freedom has been provided. We will not receive more than we ever thought possible if we are controlled by fear.

Until the boxing match between fear and freedom ends in your life, audacious generosity will not be likely.

FORGIVENESS IS GOD'S PATHWAY TO FREEDOM FROM FEAR

Allow me to go a little deeper in the forgiveness exercise I shared in chapter 4. I want to make sure you know how to live in biblical forgiveness. You need to understand how forgiveness or unforgiveness determines whether fear or freedom wins the boxing match in our lives.

During the session in which my friends walked me through biblical forgiveness, the Holy Spirit brought to mind about forty people I needed to forgive. The majority of those on my list were from the church that had fired me. The hardest to forgive were my dad, myself, and false expectations toward God.

I was upset at God for allowing me to be fired. I felt betrayed and rejected. It was interesting how fear, guilt, and rejection all surfaced. My dad screaming at me, "Kevin, you will never amount to anything" certainly had made me feel rejected. Obviously, most of the others on my list had as well, but it wasn't until I forgave my dad that the stronghold of rejection was broken in my life. I remember going into that time of prayer hemorrhaging in pain. I was so angry. I'm here to tell you, I came out of that time of prayer a free man.

It was also impactful to forgive myself. I struggled with so much shame. We can't hide from God or ourselves. When God forgives us, we are forgiven. He separates us from our sin as far as the East is from the West (Psalm 103:12). He does not recognize us by our sin, even though we often still do. It was monumental for me to forgive myself. My friends kept asking me, "Do you think you are greater than Almighty God? If He has forgiven you, then who are you to refuse to forgive yourself?" It was a real battle, but eventually, I truly forgave myself just as Christ had forgiven me. I agreed to live with the consequences, not to seek revenge, and I chose to forgive.

I renounced every lie of fear, guilt, and rejection and affirmed the gospel truth of my total security, significance, and acceptance in Christ. The boxing match was over.

Since then, there have been times that the enemy wants me to enter back into the boxing match. But it has been replaced by the truth and grace of God, so it always backfires in the enemy's face. Can I still experience fear, guilt, and rejection? Absolutely. But now it doesn't stick. Now my life is characterized by my security, significance, and acceptance in Christ.

Worship is one of my weapons. Now I respond to temptation with thanksgiving, and it is amazing how thanksgiving will shut down the enemy's schemes.

There is another important word that goes hand in hand with forgiveness, and that is belief.

I encourage you to offer yourself the same **forgiveness** God has given to you. Set yourself free from your past. God has, so you should too. Once you have forgiven yourself, **believe** the truth, and never stop believing. Becoming a Believer at salvation is not a "been there, done that" one-time occurrence. It is a lifelong commitment. Be a Believer. Believe God is who He says He is and will do what He says He will do. Believe who God has made you to be in Christ. Believe the truth that you are now secure, accepted, and significant. Every morning, affirm your identity in Christ.

I have no shortage of belief that Jesus is holy, righteous, and a delight to the Father. But I did see myself as disgraceful and disgusting to the Father. So, one day, I put myself literally in Christ. I put a picture of myself in my Bible. Guess what I saw once I closed my Bible? I saw the Bible. I saw Jesus, the Word that became flesh and dwelled among us. I couldn't see myself. I saw God's holiness and righteousness. It was then that I began to see myself as my Heavenly Father sees me. Try it. Put yourself in Christ. Your heavenly Father has, so you can too. This will set you free.

The benefit of ending the boxing match between fear and freedom is how it illuminates the presence of God in your life. Nothing honors God more than for you to experience, receive, and give all He has for you.

Let me show you how this relates to audacious generosity. Imagine that you came across a person who is suffering from severe hunger, and you gave them a provision of food that would never run out. Imagine how life-changing that would be for them. They would never starve again. They no longer would struggle to survive, but instead, they could thrive. They could grow stronger. They could be healthy in every way. Not only would this provision of food be just for them, but they could share it with anyone and everyone who would accept it. Not only do they get to eat, but now they can be generous. All of a sudden, their life can have purpose and meaning. Now they could have a mission and reason to live. Wouldn't it be sad if they just kept starving? That's what it is like when God sets us free, but we remain in fear.

The second step toward audacious generosity is setting yourself free. We need to set ourselves free because expectations matter and impact audacious generosity. Once your boxing match ends with you living in freedom, it's time to move on to the next match. In the next chapter, we're going to tackle how to end the boxing match between working versus resting.

CHAPTER 8

WORKING VERSUS RESTING

Do you focus more on working or resting? In my experience, most people focus on working.

I was no different. In fact, this boxing match nearly killed me, my marriage, and my ministry. It's even drawn me close to quitting the ministry. You have no idea how many times I found myself resenting the term "abundant life." I felt enslaved to having to perform to appease God. As a minister of the gospel of Jesus Christ, I wanted to do great things for Him.

I'm guessing you can relate. Most of us have expected to be more and do more. I used to hear the saying, "If it is to be, then it is up to me." So my sixty-hour workweek as a church planter became seventy, eighty, even ninety hours per week. Few things are more hellacious than to be a child of God enslaved to a performance trap that depends on the work we do.

I wish someone would have sat me down and said, "We are born with the expectation to work. At the moment, we take Jesus only for salvation, the expectations shift from working to resting." Perhaps it would have changed my life if someone had said, "In Christ, you are already everything God expects of you." My life might have turned out differently if someone had said, "God is great and doesn't need us to do great work for Him."

JESUS PROMISES REST

Listen to how these verses call us to rest. Psalm 46:10 says, "Be still, and know that I am God," (NIV). Isaiah 30:15 (NLT) reads, "This is what the Sovereign Lord says: 'Only in returning to me and resting in me will you be saved. In quietness and confidence is your strength.'" My favorite example is Matthew 11:28, Jesus said, "Come to me, all of you who are weary and carry heavy burdens, and I will give you rest," (NLT).

What kind of rest was Jesus talking about there? He's talking about a rest from depending on our work or from what we can produce. If we are not careful, we will continue in the old system of measuring success by our work. Salvation is all about the work God has done through Christ. We do nothing. It has nothing to do with our work. It is all God's work. In fact, we are God's work.

Freeing yourself from the boxing match between working versus resting frees you to live expectantly from God. Living expectantly from God is a life full of confident hope of receiving His blessings.

It is critical that you set yourself free to rest instead of work. This was a painful process for me and at times I still struggle to live free to rest instead of work. Yes, we must work hard in life, but understand that the work of God is done. Set yourself free from the expectation that your life depends on your work. We must take courage to live expectantly by resting in the work of God.

Years ago as I was finding freedom in Christ, God led me to fill up my journal with the theme, *Only God Works*. I recorded the life-changing experience of realizing that it is God who works in us to accomplish the work He wants done. As Paul says, he was the chief of all sinners. I can say, "Me too." And I'd add, "I was the chief of insecure workaholics for God."

When I was going through the conflict with the new leaders of the church I had planted, I journaled how my body ached from head to toe. I had more sickness that year than in the previous ten years combined. I worked ninety hours some weeks. I'd finally get to bed around 3:30 a.m. and would get up at 6:30 a.m. to help get the kids ready for school. I didn't even drink coffee then.

I had two kidney stones that year because my diet consisted of a Mountain Dew and Snickers for breakfast. I lived on decongestants around the clock to counter all my sinus infections. I was sleep-deprived and living in a constant state of self-induced dehydration. Since I wasn't feeling well, I decided I would get a flu shot. Unfortunately, my immune system was so compromised, I still ended up having three rounds of the flu that year. Even with high fevers, I would continue to work. When I say I nearly allowed the work of God to kill me, I mean it. I suffered. My wife suffered. Our family suffered. It was horrible. Even now, I can't look back and laugh about it. It was a living hell.

After the church voted to dismiss me as their pastor, I remember sharing my pain with a group of pastors. They all prayed with me, and after the gathering, one of the men that I'd never met followed me to my car and said, "Perhaps you've not been fired. Perhaps you've just been set free." I didn't appreciate it then, but I look back now and see how prophetic that was.

Wow. Did God ever have His work cut out for Him. Not only did I need to be set free from fear, guilt, and rejection, but I desperately needed to be set free from working my tail off for God. I needed to be set free from working. This represented an incredible boxing match in my life. I had no freedom to rest. It was like there were satanic scales over my eyes. I had no comprehension of how to be still and know that He is God.

I will never forget when the light bulb finally came on for me—on the plane ride back from India when I drew that second cross in my journal and committed to pursue the presence of God first and foremost in my life. I knew "the need," but I didn't know "the how." I struggled to find rest. All I knew was hard work. It's what I thought God expected of me, but my expectations were all wrong.

Over the next year, the Holy Spirit schooled me in the reality that only God works. What I learned is that we are the work of God. My work will not remain. Only the work of God through me will remain. The things God wants done are things only God can do. Only God can convict someone of sin. Only God can reveal Himself to people. Only God can empower someone to obey Him. Only God can forgive sin. Only God can reconcile. Only God can restore. What matters is not the work of our hands, but His work in and through us. The earth and everything in it has been made by Him and for Him (John 1:3, Colossians 1:16). Unless God is at work, there is nothing of eternal value to remain. God opened up my eyes, my heart, and my understanding that only God works (Philippians 2:13).

This was life-changing for me. The more I realize that only God works, the more I am committed to pursue the presence of God. The more I sit in God's presence, the greater my sense of mission. I started seeing God's mission through the expectation of freedom.

RESIGN FROM WORKING

I have since resigned from working. I encourage you to resign from working too. This doesn't mean you become lazy. Nothing could be further from the truth. Sometimes we resist teaching grace, thinking it will only give people a license to sin. The more grace we experience and receive, the less desire we have to continue in sin. The same is true for freedom from work.

My life is very full and busy. Instead of depending on what I can produce, now the fruit of God's work happens naturally through me.

A lot has happened in the twenty years after my first trip to India in 1998. For three years, I served at the counseling ministry for pastors. Then, for seven years, I was busy distributing food and needed resources through what became known as With Love from Jesus Ministries (WLFJ). When God called me away from that, I started a company called Freedom Managers. I sold Freedom Managers a few years later and joined the staff at Hope Community Church in

Raleigh, North Carolina, and served there for three years before God called me to focus on Global Hope India full time.

I've now traveled over one million miles to twenty-seven different countries. I've been to India over fifty times. I've taken 1,000 people on short-term mission trips to India. We've raised millions for God's work among Indian Nationals. I invest my time into our Indian partners and hosting our short-term mission teams while they are on the ground in India. In the USA, I invest in our board of directors, the Global Hope India staff, and local leaders.

My family is very important to me. I constantly invest time and hard work into my wife, our family, and our home. Shelly and I have been married for thirty-three years. We have three adult children and one granddaughter.

I lead a Bible study group in our home (or on Zoom) every Monday evening. I volunteer every Sunday from 6 a.m. to 2 p.m. at church. I host two podcast shows. I'd say my life's pretty busy!

Thankfully, I'm not the same workaholic I used to be. Over the last two decades, I have averaged at least seven to eight hours of sleep per night. My health has improved significantly. I am hydrated, and I've had no more kidney stones. I have even completed four half Ironman events, one being in Chennai, India.

My productivity has dramatically increased. The greatest difference is that I am enjoying a living relationship with God, whereby He works in and through me. The work no longer depends on me. Hallelujah! I am free to be a child of God. I'm not afraid to close my laptop. I'm free to be more aware of the people around me and no longer see them as a distraction. I am free to pursue God's presence first and foremost in my life.

Another difference is the fascinating life of audacious generosity I am allowed to live. Sometimes God will produce more fruit through me in a single day than I used to produce the whole time I was working so hard to plant a church.

What I have learned is that there is no limit to what God can produce when we rest in Him. The benefit of ending the boxing match between working versus resting is rest.

So, what about you? Is your life more characterized by working or resting?

CHARACTERIZED BY RESTING

Ending the boxing match between working versus resting is not pretending that life doesn't take work. It does. The question is, which characterizes us? Are we more characterized by working or by resting?

Being healthy takes work. Getting the right amount of nutrition, sleep, and exercise takes work. Wearing clean clothing takes work. Staying well-groomed takes work. Being married takes work. Raising children takes work. It takes time to invest in a living relationship with God, to pray, read the Bible, meditate, and worship. Know that I am cheering you on for every investment you make into your relationship with God.

No matter your age, marital status, or season of life, there is always work to be done. I'm not asking you if you work. My point is not to condemn you for being a hard worker. Actually, I applaud and praise you for every investment you are making into the lives of others.

It is absolutely possible to work hard from a place of resting. We will all have nights and even seasons where we have no control over our physical rest, but even then, we can still be characterized by resting. We can be characterized by resting even while bringing a newborn home from the hospital. I know working versus resting can be a mix of gore and glory. I believe our life should depend upon God and not ourselves. We should be able to rest from our work. We should take time to be in God's presence. We should have freedom to be loved by God.

Resting comes from what you expect from God. If you expect that your life depends upon your work, then you have no choice but to endure a life of endless work. Instead, let God work. Depend on His work, not your work. Rest. If you expect that your life depends on God, then you'll be free to rest. If you look for it, you will find endless invitations from God to rest in His work. I encourage you to rest. Breathe. Relax.

LOVE YOURSELF AS GOD LOVES YOU

In order to set yourself free, you have to love yourself the way that your heavenly Father loves you. God absolutely loves us while absolutely hating our sins. You can, too. You can love yourself as a creation and child of God. You can hate your sin. The gospel is that nothing can cause God to love you more. Nothing can cause God to love you less. God loves you. Setting yourself free involves loving yourself with the love you have received from God.

If you read Jesus' prayer to the Father in John 17, you can see how much the Father loves the Son and how much the Son loves the Father. There is so much love in the Trinity, it overflows into all our lives. Jesus is basically modeling love for us in the Trinity. This is the kind of love that produces audacious generosity. God is characterized by generosity. There is no selfishness or greed in Him.

Ask yourself this question: **Do I give myself the same love God gives me?** For the longest time, my answer was no. I want you to experience and receive God's love. God loves you so you can love yourself.

Audacious generosity is far from passive. God took action. He loved so, He gave the greatest possession He has—His very own presence. **Audacious generosity requires love in action.** Too often, we think of love in action as it relates to us loving others. I encourage you to consider the love you need to show yourself. I'm not talking about just giving yourself warm fuzzies. I'm talking about setting yourself free from your past. I'm talking about you offering yourself the same forgiveness God has given you.

In Matthew 22:36-40, Jesus is asked, What is the most important commandment? We read, "Jesus replied, 'You must love the Lord your God with all your heart, all your soul, and all your mind.' This is the first and greatest commandment. A second is equally important: 'Love your neighbor as yourself,'" (NLT).

It is easy to see two people we are required to love: God and others. It includes a third person we are to love: ourselves. Jesus says, "Love your neighbor as yourself." Jesus said it in such a way it indicates that love for ourselves is assumed.

It is important to understand that human love is different from God's love. Human love for ourselves needs to be upgraded to God's love. The Bible uses the word *Agape* for God's love. *Agape* love is the highest form of love as it refers to God's pure, willful, and sacrificial love. There is a difference. We can be confused by calling both love. We all know people who say they love others, but their actions are selfish and greedy. Often, we think we have to hate ourselves in order to selflessly love others. This is not true or even possible.

Actually, Jesus is ordering it this way: we must first love God, then love ourselves, and third, love others. We can't love others until we have loved ourselves enough to free ourselves. This is a God-honoring love for ourselves. It's a love aligned with God's Word. As God has set us free, then we need to love ourselves enough to receive that freedom. This love is generous and produces generosity. It doesn't foster selfishness and greed as with carnal love. We can't hate ourselves and go love people. You can't hate yourself and be generous to others.

FORGIVING YOURSELF IS GOD'S PATHWAY TO FREEING YOURSELF

In the last chapter, I walked you through biblical forgiveness. I shared how impactful it was for me to forgive myself. God's forgiveness is one of the most loving things He will ever do for us. The same is true of us. Forgiving ourselves is the most loving thing we'll ever do for ourselves. We free ourselves by applying Jesus' work on the cross. We do it by aligning ourselves to the Word of God. We free ourselves by forgiving ourselves as God has forgiven us.

If you haven't already, I encourage you to forgive yourself.

Agree to live with the consequences, not to seek revenge, and choose to forgive yourself. Renounce every lie of fear, guilt, and rejection as a result of your past. Affirm the truth of your security, significance, and acceptance in Christ.

When you forgive yourself, you separate yourself from your sins just like God does. This is the only way to hate your sins and still love yourself. When you forgive yourself, you free yourself from your past just like God does. In Christ, your past is GONE. This is how you set yourself free. This is what it takes for us to rest. Until we forgive ourselves, we have no choice but to work in our attempt to survive and thrive. This is not God's plan or provision.

Forgiving yourself is God's path to you setting yourself free. This enables you to rest. Finally, the boxing match is over.

Audacious generosity happens when God is the Giver, and giving depends on what He gives through you. Audacious generosity depends on what God produces, not on what you can produce. This is true in having a living relationship with God. And it's true when it comes to working or resting. Set yourself free to rest.

The second step toward audacious generosity is setting yourself free. When the boxing match of fear versus freedom ends, it is absolutely life-changing. When you end the boxing match of working versus resting, it is completely and incredibly freeing. If that's not enough, it still gets better. In the next chapter, we'll tackle how to end the boxing match between reprimand and reward. It's time for you to expect to be rewarded by God instead of reprimanded by God.

CHAPTER 9

REPRIMAND VERSUS REWARD

Do you expect God to reprimand you or to reward you? If you said reprimand, you're not alone. I did. Most people are waiting for God to reprimand them. I can't tell you how badly I struggled with this one. Talk about a knock-down, drag-out boxing match. This is perhaps the heavyweight title match of all time.

PEOPLE NEED REWARDS, NOT REPRIMANDS

Audacious generosity is not possible if all we have to offer is reprimand. Ain't nobody got time for that. God forbid we become more generous in reprimanding others. You can't expect God to reprimand you, and then somehow have this life of audacious generosity in rewarding others. Wouldn't that be the ultimate contradiction? We can't give what we haven't received, otherwise, we are just offering a knock-off version. That is not audacious generosity.

Today, my expectations have changed. In fact, I wouldn't be writing this if I didn't believe with all my heart that our loving Heavenly Father wants nothing more than to reward you. Actually, He is grieved when we walk around, expecting to be reprimanded.

Ending this boxing match between being reprimanded or rewarded is important because both result in receiving from God. I want you to think about the opportunity I'm sharing with you in the context of how to experience, receive, and give more than you ever thought possible.

At the end of this section, I'm going to walk you through the steps to free yourself so that you can receive more than you ever thought possible. Before we get there, however, I need you to seriously consider what you expect to receive from God.

For years I expected to receive reprimand from God. I expected to get what I deserved. My expectations were focused on my behavior and not on my Savior. It wasn't until I started depending on the work of God, instead of depending on my work that I was free to replace the expectation to be reprimanded with the expectation to be rewarded. Notice how important resting from our work is. Depending on the law or our own efforts instead of grace will always foster the expectation to be reprimanded.

Had it not been for Christ, we would deserve to be reprimanded. We know the Father loves the Son and desires to reward Him. The Father has promised to exalt The Son and reward His work on the cross. The work of God always deserves to be rewarded.

Earlier I wrote that I put a photo of myself into my Bible to illustrate being alive in Christ. As I closed my Bible, all I could see was Jesus and His holiness. I couldn't see my sinful self any longer. The same is true for reward. We are alive in Christ. How can the Father reward the Son and we not benefit? He can't. We will always benefit as a result of our association in Christ.

Have you ever been upgraded on an airplane because of an association you had? Have you ever walked through doors you didn't expect? Have you ever met someone you would never expect to meet except for the person you were with?

I will never forget in May 2009, walking into AT&T Stadium in Arlington, Texas. The stadium had just opened as the home of the Dallas Cowboys of the National Football League (NFL). This stadium is known for its retractable roof. It offers a one-of-a-kind experience unlike any other stadium in the world. The stadium seats 80,000, making it the fourth largest stadium in the NFL by seating capacity. The maximum capacity of the stadium with standing room is 105,000. It also has the world's twenty-nineth largest high definition video screens, which hang from one twenty-yard line to the other twenty-yard line. I know many people who have added a visit to this iconic stadium onto their bucket list.

Within a year of AT&T Stadium opening, I played a brief game of football with some friends on the field. I was not just visiting, but playing football during a private tour on the field. I toured the locker rooms, saw how the team buses drive in underneath the stadium, and even sat in one of the lounges.

I didn't pay a dime for this private tour. My admission into the stadium had nothing to do with me. It had to do with who I was with. One of the men in our group had the right connections who made the right phone calls to the right person. I got to stand on the iconic Dallas Cowboy star painted on the fifty-yard line. I have cheered for the Cowboys (and their cheerleaders) since I was in middle school. This was a dream come true.

We've all known the joy of walking through doors we'd likely never get through on our own. We've all sat in seats we didn't deserve to sit in. We've all enjoyed the privileges of others. I'm paraphrasing, but Scripture says if we who are evil know how to upgrade one another, how much more does our Heavenly Father know how to upgrade us (Matthew 7:11.). Almighty God can't upgrade the Son without those in Christ being upgraded too. This includes you.

Most people have no difficulty accepting the Father's desire and plan to reward the Son. We struggle to expect God to reward us. Through forgiveness, God has committed Himself to never seek revenge. He has agreed to live with the consequences. He has chosen to forgive. The threat of reprimand is over. It's gone. Now I want you to end the boxing match between reprimand and reward in your life. It is over.

Ending this boxing match can be a struggle. The Apostle Paul identifies this struggle in Romans 6, 7, and 8. I wish a brother in Christ would have told me twenty years ago about how big of a struggle this boxing match could be:

In 1999, we opened our home up to a nine-year-old foster son. His dad had passed away a year earlier, and his mom was in the hospital. His family asked us to take him in for two weeks, but we ended up raising him for three years. Six weeks after coming into our home, his mother passed away. I was the one who knelt beside Scott and told him his mother was gone. I held him as we cried together. I officiated his mom's funeral. All he had known his whole life was trauma.

A few weeks before he came to live with us, we picked him up from a behavioral management hospital. That weekend, we went to a local Christmas parade. He sat there on the curb like a zombie staring out into space because he was so deeply medicated. Earlier his behavior was so bad he was diagnosed as bipolar and prescribed high doses of antidepressants and mood-altering medications in order to control him.

I remember the doctors asking me, "Do you know what you're getting yourself into?" Knowing God had led us to bring him into our home, I felt completely safe. To me, he was a nine-year-old boy in crisis. Our biological children were eleven, eight, and five. I thought, "What's one more child to raise?" We loved Scott like our own.

Within a few months, we worked with his healthcare providers to reduce his medicine. For the first year, we were like in a honeymoon stage as Scott was experiencing so many firsts. Every time we did something as a family, he would tell us how it was the first time he had ever done that. It was the first time he had gone fishing, baked cookies, gone to SeaWorld, stayed in a hotel, and even had a brother and sisters.

Soon he began acting out. I remember having to say to him over and over and over, "Scott, you are safe now." Again and again, he would revert to being scared. He expected to be reprimanded. Earlier, he had been physically, emotionally, and sexually abused. He knew language most sailors don't even use. Even a year after being in a safe and loving home with our family, he still expected to be abused and neglected.

Scott lived with us for three years until he and his family decided he would live with his grandmother. The time in our home was a stabilizing refuge for him. Scott actually took Jesus only for salvation while he lived with us. Praise the Lord.

Still, this experience was not easy on our family. God gave us grace each step of the way. It was difficult to see this boxing match unfold in Scott's life between his past and his present. In the past, he was abused and traumatized. In our home, he was safe and loved. It took several years to slowly replace the expectations of reprimand with the expectations of reward.

Now Scott is all grown up and has his own family. I'm thankful anytime we get to catch up with one another.

My heart goes out to anyone whose life has been a struggle. I know from firsthand experience the painful struggle of pivoting from expecting reprimand to expecting reward.

I grew up with that struggle. I basically lived alone from

ages twelve to fourteen. My parents divorced, and my mom took my younger brother and sister with her. I was told to stay with my father and older brother. My father worked in town thirty minutes from where we lived, and he would often stay in town with his friends after work. My older brother was sixteen and had his driver's license, so he was gone most of the time. Each morning, my father would drop me off at school on his way to work, and in the afternoon, I would ride the bus home and be alone until I went to bed. The next morning my father would be there and drop me back off at school. This happened every day for the next two years. I taught myself how to cook, clean, and survive.

I know what it feels like to be neglected. Expecting to be neglected has strained my relationship with God. The enemy is constantly tempting me to fear what I receive or don't receive from God. The fear of being neglected used to come very quickly to me. I didn't even have to go looking for it. It was always right there in my face.

Today, the expectation of reward allows me to pivot from the enemy's temptations to thanksgiving. I try to quickly turn the temptation of fear into a time of counting my blessings. I have to discipline myself to remember how God has faithfully cared for me. God is so honored every time I give thanks. He is dishonored when I act neglected in spite of His faithfulness.

Isn't it time the enemy's schemes backfire on Him? In Genesis 50:20, Joseph said to his brothers, "You intended to harm me, but God intended it all for good," (NLT). Expecting God's reward enables us to turn temptation from the enemy into worship. All of a sudden, we see our loving Heavenly Father using the enemy to call us into worship, to give thanks, and to expect to be rewarded by God. How cool is that?

OUR IDENTITY IN CHRIST

Another important aspect is our identity in Christ. Our identity in Christ matters in whether we expect to be reprimanded or rewarded by God. I used to see myself as sinful, unholy, and a disgrace to God. At the same time, I saw Jesus as holy, righteous, and the satisfaction of God. Then I was led through a study of all the references to "in Christ" in the Bible. The Bible says we are alive in Christ (Ephesians 2:5). We are holy in Christ (1 Corinthians 1:30). We are blameless in Christ (Colossians 1:22).

In the Parable of the Prodigal Son (Luke 15:11-32), Jesus demonstrates how the character of God is to reward prodigals, not reprimand them. Let's face it; we have all been prodigals. We all deserve to be reprimanded. The good news of the gospel is that God isn't seeing our sin. He sees the blood of His son.

Ending the boxing match between reprimand and reward

allowed me to see that I have been made alive to God in Christ. I began to expect God to see Jesus in me and not my sinfulness. Slowly, my expectations changed from expecting to be reprimanded all the time to expecting to be rewarded. God's salvation and His rewards depend on Christ, not on us. If you are alive in Christ, then the expectation of being reprimanded by God is gone. That boxing match doesn't exist unless we continue to expect to be reprimanded instead of rewarded by God.

Allow me to make it clear, by expecting to be rewarded, I'm not saying we are entitled to be rewarded. Let us refuse to be infected with entitlement. It is our job to seek God's presence. Leave the rewarding up to God. I'm saying we can trust God to reward us.

Set yourself free from the expectation to be reprimanded instead of rewarded. Take courage to live expectantly of God's reward.

Listen to 1 John 4:18, "Such love has no fear because perfect love expels all fear. If we are afraid, it is for fear of punishment, and this shows that we have not fully experienced His perfect love," (NLT).

Wow. That makes so much sense now, doesn't it?

Who are we to supersede Almighty God by keeping ourselves enslaved to the wrong set of expectations? On the authority of God's Word: God has set you free. Today, I want you to take the courage to live expectantly from God and live free.

IT'S OVER

It is important for us to accept that the boxing match between reprimand and reward is over. Jesus won that battle and paid the price for our sin at the cross. He rose victorious, taking away any need for us to be reprimanded.

The benefit of ending the boxing match is it opens the door to receive God's rewards. Scripture offers very clear promises from God to reward us.

Jeremiah 17:10 used to frighten me. "But I, the Lord, search all hearts and examine secret motives. I give all people their due rewards, according to what their actions deserve," (NLT). This doesn't frighten me anymore. I now understand that God's eyes are on us to reward us, not to reprimand us. That is good news!

CHRIST PROMISED TO REWARD YOU

FOR THESE TEN THINGS:

1. Prayer and Fasting (Matthew 6:6, 17-18, Hebrews 11:6)
2. Extending compassion to the vulnerable (Matthew 25:37-40)
3. Bearing insults and being persecuted for Christ (Luke 6:22-23, Romans 8:38-39)
4. Loving your enemies (Luke 6:35, Luke 23:34)
5. Giving generously (Luke 6:38, James 1:17)
6. Hospitality that cannot be repaid (Luke 14:12-14)
7. Endurance through pressures in life (2 Corinthians 4:17-18)
8. Quality work for your employer (Colossians 3:23-24)
9. Faithfulness through trials (1 Peter 1:6-7)
10. Faithfulness to the truth (2 John 1:7-8, John 14:6)

These ten actions are all great investment opportunities to be rewarded. God makes it clear what will be rewarded, so go "all out." This is audacious generosity.

Expectations matter. It is God's good, perfect, and pleasing will for you to expect to be rewarded. Christ's work on the cross removes the fear of reprimand. You can set yourself free. In Christ, you have no past. God isn't holding your past over you. You shouldn't either.

The second step toward audacious generosity is setting yourself free. Be free to live expectantly to receive more from God than you ever thought possible. In the next chapter, we'll walk through some practical applications to further help you set yourself free.

CHAPTER 10

APPLICATION

SET YOURSELF FREE—LIVE EXPECTANTLY TO RECEIVE MORE

Have you ever been a slave? It is too easy for all of us to be enslaved to our past.

I remember being told to let Jesus forgive me of all my sins. I don't remember being encouraged to let God completely change my expectations. Even after salvation, I still expected fear instead of freedom. I still expected work instead of rest. I still expected reprimand instead of reward.

Unfortunately, those expectations stifled my relationship with God. As far as God was concerned, I was free. As far as I was concerned, however, I was still enslaved to my negative expectations. The reason I wasn't experiencing freedom was because I was holding on to the improper expectations, which were contrary to my identity in Christ. As I forgave myself and set myself free, my expectations changed. I started to live expectantly of the positive. I began to receive more from God than I ever thought possible.

Expectations matter.

SETTING YOURSELF FREE

The second step in audacious generosity that we've looked at is this concept of setting yourself free. Allowing God to change your expectations will put you on a path of living expectantly from God. Living expectantly allows you to receive more from God than you ever thought possible.

Let me walk you through three specific applications with key verses from God's Word that will move you from slavery to freedom.

APPLICATION #1: CHOOSE TO FORGIVE YOURSELF

I want you to walk yourself through the same biblical forgiveness God has given to you. Remember when God forgave your sins? Remember how God agreed to live with the consequences of your sins, how He agreed to no longer take revenge? He chose to forgive.

I want you to take a blank sheet of paper from your journal. I want you to pray and ask the Holy Spirit to bring to mind any choices, mistakes, or sins you're holding against yourself. It can be something committed by you or against you. For example, sometimes victims of rape hold the rape against themselves long after they forgive their rapist. I remember blaming myself for my parents' divorce. Let the Holy Spirit bring to mind anything for which you need to forgive yourself. Think through what causes you to experience shame, anger, guilt, and rejection. Add those to the list. Take as much time as you need to make your list.

Now, one-by-one, I want you to pray and agree to live with the consequences of your choices, mistakes, and sins. Agree to no longer seek revenge against yourself. Don't beat yourself up anymore. I want you to choose to forgive. Say it out loud: I here and now choose to forgive myself for _____. Keep going one-by-one through your whole list.

Take time to meditate on John 20:23. Understand how this applies to you forgiving your sins too. The implication is that if we refuse to forgive ourselves, it will prevent us from experiencing the truth of God's forgiveness. The opposite is true. Forgiving ourselves frees us to experience God's forgiveness. Now that's truly setting yourself free.

Key Verse: If you forgive anyone's sins, they are forgiven. If you do not forgive them, they are not forgiven (John 20:23) (NLT).

The Point: Offer yourself the same forgiveness God has given you.

APPLICATION #2: SURRENDER YOUR PAST TO GOD

Take the list of sins for which you just forgave yourself, and at the top in bold letters write, "My Past." On a new page in your journal, I want you to also write, "My Past" at the top. I want you to compare the two sheets. The one showing the list of sins reminds you of your past sins. The blank one with only the words "My Past" illustrates what God sees.

I want you to destroy the one listing all your sins. Rip it up. Crumble it into a tiny ball, and throw it away. Now reflect on the blank one that God sees. One of the greatest realities of our freedom in Christ is that in Christ, we have no past. The past is forgiven. The past is gone. That's freedom. Now I want you to celebrate. You can throw a party as big as you want. I hope you'll shout! I encourage you to have a piece of cake or something tangible to celebrate.

Key Verse: This means that anyone who belongs to Christ has become a new person. The old life is gone; a new life has begun (2 Corinthians 5:17) (NLT).

The Point: Celebrate that Christ has freed you from your past.

These steps were the most difficult for me. I still have to let go of my past on a regular basis. Now we need to get rid of any lies.

APPLICATION #3: EXCHANGE LIES FOR TRUTH

In this application, we will exchange negative lies for positive truth. Open to a blank page in your journal and allow the Holy Spirit to bring to mind any messages that are not from God. Think of any negative self-talk. For me, it was my father saying, "Kevin, you will never amount to anything." This represented the lie of rejection in my life. Other examples of negative self-talk include: *I am ugly. I am fat. I am dyslexic. Nobody likes me. I don't have what it takes. I'm not worthy.* You might think of one or one hundred. Ask the Holy Spirit to reveal to you every lie that rolls around in your mind. Wait until no more come to mind.

Now, one-by-one, I want you to renounce out loud every lie. I want you to immediately affirm the truth found in Psalm 139:14, "I am fearfully and wonderfully made," (NIV). For example, I would say, "I renounce the lie that I will never amount to anything. I affirm the truth that I am fearfully and wonderfully made" or "I renounce the lie that I am worthless. I affirm the truth I am fearfully and wonderfully made." Repeat this process until you are all the way through your list.

Next, ask the Holy Spirit to reveal any identity that you feel like others have given you or that you have given yourself. Perhaps people have called you mean, stupid, or selfish. Perhaps you say things like that to yourself. Create your list and then, one-by-one, renounce out loud every false identity and immediately affirm the truth of your identity in Christ. For example, I would say, "I renounce the false identity of being consumed with myself. I affirm the truth that in Christ, I am consumed with God and others." Another example: "I renounce the false identity of being a jerk. I affirm the truth that in Christ, I am a kind and considerate person." Repeat this process for every false identity the Holy Spirit brings to mind. Come out of this time of prayer, standing tall in your identity in Christ.

Key Verse: They exchanged the truth about God for a lie and worshiped and served created things rather than the Creator—who is forever praised. Amen (Romans 1:25) (NIV).

The Point: From this day forward, I want you to exchange lies for truth. When you exchange lies for truth, what you're doing is exchanging negative expectations for positive expectations, which allows you to live expectantly from God.

I pray you're already feeling freer. Keep in mind our freedom in Christ is derived from the Word of God and not our feelings. Allow your emotions time to catch up with the truth. It really doesn't matter what you feel. What matters is that you receive God's work of freedom in your life.

CONGRATULATIONS ON SETTING YOURSELF FREE

Making these three applications enables you to set yourself free. Living expectantly from God frees you from your life, depending on what you can produce. Now you are free to depend on what God can produce. This is the life God has always wanted for you.

Here are three additional exchanges I want you to make that relate to audacious generosity:

1. Renounce the lie that giving is a "have to." Affirm the truth that giving is a "get to."
2. Renounce the lie that your life depends on what you can produce. Affirm the truth that your life depends on what God can produce.
3. Renounce the lie that God depends on what you can give. Affirm the truth that God is the Giver and that giving depends upon what God gives through you.

LIVING EXPECTANTLY TO RECEIVE MORE

I encourage you to be as confident about God's care of you

as He is. Give yourself permission to expect to receive more from God than you ever thought possible. Commit to the journey of audacious generosity.

Setting God and myself free changed my life. Setting others free changed my giving. The third step toward audacious generosity is setting others free, which we'll dive into next.

SECTION 3

SET OTHERS FREE

CHAPTER 11

LIVE GENEROUSLY TO GIVE MORE

The key is in your hands. I suspect all of us can remember asking others where something is only to find it in our hands. This "aha" moment awaits when it comes to setting others free.

This is where things get good. The reason God sets us free is to equip and empower us to free Him, ourselves, and others. While it is a joy to experience and receive, Jesus promises that we are even more blessed when we give (Acts 20:35). Jesus is pointing to where the greatest blessings from God are reserved. We all want to be blessed. Few of us wake up in the morning, longing to give. We need to change that.

When an offering plate is passed on earth and we say, "Oh no," in heaven, they are cheering, "Oh yes!" because they know the blessings that come through giving. By the end of this section, I hope you will never look at an offering plate, beggar, or opportunity to give the same way. I want you to understand why God loves a cheerful giver (2 Corinthians 9:6-7). More importantly, I want you to wake up every morning ready to be a cheerful giver.

STEP #3: SET OTHERS FREE

In this section, we're going to look at what it means to set others free. It is important for us to set others free in order to live generously. I am convinced if someone gave you a million dollars to give away and instructed you with their values, you would have the best time of your life giving it all away. It would bring purpose and meaning to your life. I am equally convinced that this is the opportunity of audacious generosity.

In the chapters that follow, I'm going to walk you through three switches that need to be flipped in order to truly set others free:

1. Get or Give
2. Greed or Generosity
3. Burden or Blessing

These three switches hold the power to either block or fuel audacious generosity. The key to setting others free is not within others. It is within us. It's not like we have gone and locked people up so now we have to go set them free. It is that we have been born into a broken and sinful world motivated to get instead of to give. We were born programmed by our sinful nature to be greedy instead of being generous. We were born seeing ourselves and others as more of a burden than a blessing.

God is ready to give you the courage and freedom necessary for you to flip these switches in your life. Flipping these switches will result in you setting others free, and allow you to live generously in order to give more than you ever thought possible. Before salvation, we are powerless in flipping these switches. At salvation, however, we are given the power of the resurrection within us to flip them, permanently locking them into a set position.

There is nothing more loving than setting others free. Galatians 5:13 says, "For you have been called to live in freedom, my brothers and sisters. But don't use your freedom to satisfy your sinful nature. Instead, use your freedom to serve one another in love," (NLT).

Setting others free is seeing others through God's eyes. Accepting, loving, and serving everyone. Offering them the very same security, acceptance, and significance that God has given you. Offering them the same freedom God has given you.

> Until we set others free, we will limit our experience of audacious generosity.

WE LOVE TO SEE GENEROSITY

We all love Oprah's Favorite Things Giveaways as she has given away cars, cash, college scholarships, and homes. We equally love Ellen DeGeneres' Greatest Nights of Giveaways. All of us have cried as Ty Pennington of the Extreme Makeover Home Edition shouted, "Move that bus!" You know the scene or one like it. The TV host goes in, convinces a worthy family to leave their home for a few days, and his team does an extreme makeover of the home. They transform it from being a rundown firetrap to a beautiful home in just a few days.

Finally, the worthy family returns home. They are standing in front of their house and a tour bus is blocking the view of their new home. The camera crew films the scene as the host shouts, "Move that bus!" Immediately everyone is crying and falling to their knees in disbelief. At that moment, millions of viewers around the world are crying tears of joy along with this family. It is a beautiful scene.

The love for generosity comes from God. No one is more generous than God. No one. Not Oprah, Bill Gates, a reality TV host, you, me, or anyone who's ever lived. Generosity is a characteristic of God. God is kind and plentiful.

> Audacious generosity is to allow God to be kind and plentiful through you.

JOHN 3:16 IS A GREAT EXAMPLE OF AUDACIOUS GENEROSITY

Let's look at John 3:16 in the original Greek language: For God so loved the world that he gave...

The English translation doesn't do justice here. The Greek word used for love is agape (agapáō). This is God's love, which we looked at in section two. One of the root meanings is "to prefer." As a follower of Christ, "to love" means actively doing what the Lord prefers. We prefer others by the power of His Spirit and with His direction. One of my favorite definitions of true "loving" is always defined by God—a "discriminating affection which involves choice and selection." For example, 1 John 4:8,16,17 conveys how "loving or preferring" Jesus is as He lives His life through His followers.

The Greek word for gave is *dídōmi*, pronounced THEE-thoh-mee. It is a verb which means to give others something to their advantage. It is used 413 times in 377 verses in the Bible. Generosity is the characteristic of God. Giving is one of God's most common actions and expectations.

The Greek language helps to broaden our understanding.

Let's bring these two Greek words together. For God possesses this discriminating affection, which involves choice and selection for the world (that's you and me) that He gives us something for our advantage (His only son, Jesus) so that whoever believes in Jesus will not perish, but live forever.

I encourage you to re-read this multiple times. I've recited John 3:16 my whole life. Adding in the meaning of these two Greek words has brought a significant upgrade to my understanding.

JESUS LOVES THE WHOLE WORLD

If the world we are willing to love is not the same as the world identified in John 3:16—which is all people—then audacious generosity is not complete.

We are not allowed to control who God can love. We can't say, "Father, flow through my life to love 'these' people; just don't make me go love 'those' people." If you are trying to reason with God about this, then perhaps you need to go back to re-read section one about setting God free to experience more. When we set God free, we agree to let God be God. We agree to love who He loves. We can't deny generosity to some people and yet somehow demonstrate audacious generosity to others.

Is there anyone you are unwilling to allow God to be generous to through you? If we are honest, we'd all have someone we are reluctant to give to. It is important to understand the whole point of John 3:16 is that God is on a mission.

GOD IS ON A MISSION

What is our Heavenly Father's work? Jesus reveals it in His mission. He says, "The Son of Man came to seek and save those who are lost" (Luke 19:10) (NLT). 2 Peter 3:9 says, "The Lord isn't really being slow about His promise, as some people think. No, He is being patient for your sake. He does not want anyone to be destroyed, but wants everyone to repent," (NLT).

God's mission is to extend His presence on the earth through salvation. God's strategy is audacious generosity.

Let's face it; the challenge about generosity is we don't like being the GIVER. We have no problem watching other people GIVE their resources to others. The problem comes when we feel like God wants us to take OUR resources and GIVE them to Him or others.

GOD IS THE GIVER

The courage for audacious generosity is found in the truth that God is the Giver, not you. This truth allows you to freely give what God puts in your hands. Colossians 1:16 says everything has been made by Him and for Him. This means we are stewards, not owners. It is our responsibility to manage, not to control or keep.

Audacious generosity occurs as we allow God to own all and give all through us.

The more we understand God's strategy of audacious generosity, the more we will appreciate the importance of setting others free.

Here is where we face the fact that God IS the Giver, and we are not.

Giving more than you ever thought possible requires pivoting from giving what you can produce to giving what God can produce.

The proportions are extremely different. You can feed your family, but only God can feed the multitude. Even if you have the capacity to feed way more than your family, God always has more multitude than your supply. There is no question that God wants to give through you. He has everything in heaven and earth at His disposal to give.

THE SECRET SAUCE

The secret to you giving more than you ever thought possible is to first experience and receive more than you ever thought possible. Setting God, yourself, and others free removes the barriers to make this possible. Freeing others not only impacts your giving, but it will also impact how much you experience and receive. The fundamental question is, why should God trust you to experience and receive more if you're not willing to give? Once you set others free as you have God and yourself, then nothing limits your giving.

If you will focus on setting others free, then giving will automatically occur as a natural result. Setting God free allows you to experience more of God than you ever thought possible. Setting yourself free allows you to receive more from God than you ever thought possible. Notice what's happening. The more of the GIVER you experience and receive, the more you will experience Him GIVING through you. You need to understand that you cannot give what you haven't received. You can't receive what you haven't experienced. Make sure you accept this progression:

Experience forgiveness—Receive forgiveness—Give Forgiveness

Experience love—Receive love—Give love

Experience freedom—Receive freedom—Give freedom

Experience grace—Receive grace—Give grace

Experience God—Receive God—Give God

Experience more—Receive more—Give more

Let's examine the posture of our hands.

LIVING OPENHANDED

It's time to get practical. God has dealt a lot with our hearts. Now let us allow Him to deal with our hands. Our hands are either a dam or a channel of God's gifts. The posture of our hands demonstrates if we have set God, ourselves, and others free.

If someone watched your hands, would they be closed, or do you live openhanded? Would we see that your hands are used to get or to give? Are your fists closed or your palms open? Do your hands depend on what you can produce or what God can produce?

We set others free and live generously for God when we let God multiply His blessings in our hands. I want you to notice that in the story of the Feeding of the Multitude, we see how Jesus broke the fish and loaves, blessed them, and gave them to the disciples to distribute (Matthew 14:19). We can assume the multiplication occurred in the disciples' hands as they were distributing the fish and loaves to the people. Matthew 14:19 seems to indicate that the multiplication did not occur in Jesus' hands.

There is another important observation to be made. The multiplication occurred as they gave it. Had the story gone: Jesus broke it, blessed it, gave it to the disciples and they ate it, that would have been the end of the story. Notice one more thing. It says, "After everyone had their fill, the disciples collected twelve basketfuls of leftovers." So the disciples certainly ate too. No one went away hungry. It was Christ in action through audacious generosity that fed the multitude.

Remember what God taught us when the miracle food began:

Hoard it and lose it. Give it and it returns.

Far too many people are measuring their success solely based on what they can earn. It's time for us to measure success by what we can give.

Too many Christians have absolutely no idea what God could give through them because they hoard it and lose it instead of giving. Even if at the end of our life we had earned $1 million, died debt-free, and left a nice inheritance to our family, wouldn't it still be a tragedy if God could have given

$100 million to missions through us during our lifetime had we just lived with audacious generosity?

As a follower of Jesus Christ, you have committed to go where He says to go and do what He says to do, right? If you didn't realize that is what it means to be a Christ-follower, then make that your commitment now. Commit to go where He says to go and do what He says to do.

One of the practical applications of what He wants us to do is to allow Him to GIVE to others through us.

GOD'S MISSION IS ADVANCED

What results in setting others free and living generously is the mission of God is advanced. As you enter this movement of audacious generosity, you'll no longer just read about the miracles in the Bible. You will experience modern-day miracles in your everyday life. Now, you will allow God to be God. Now, you will allow God to use your hands to be generous. Now, you are free to experience, receive, and give more than you ever thought possible. Now, by setting others free, there is nothing keeping you from audacious generosity.

The dam has been broken. The channel is open. God can flow in and through you to reveal Himself in the midst of human need. Now, your giving is not limited to what you can produce. Now, your giving is not about you at all. Can you see what's happening?

> If we can eliminate fear and know freedom where nothing prevents God from using us, then there is no limit to audacious generosity.

God is on a mission, and His strategy for fulfilling it is audacious generosity. God is the Giver. We are His hands and feet. God wants to give generously through us as we set others free.

Nothing holds you back from freely giving anything and everything God puts into your hands to anyone and everyone. Get this connection:

> Courage affords you freedom. Freedom affords you audacious generosity.

The third step toward audacious generosity is setting others free. Living generously for God allows you to give more than you ever thought possible. We need to set others free so that our world matches God's world as seen in John 3:16.

It starts with committing to live with the purpose to give.

CHAPTER 12

GET OR GIVE?

I want to offer you a gift I wish someone had offered me. When I was going through my transformation from fear to freedom, I wish someone had encouraged me to abandon my need to GET more for God's opportunity to GIVE more. Perhaps it would not have taken me as many years to flip the switch from getting more to giving more.

We are all born with the obsession to get more. At salvation, we are offered a different purpose for our life. We are offered the opportunity to start giving more than we ever thought possible. After salvation, we have the richest and most generous person in the world living inside of us. The same power that raised Jesus from the dead is available to us, too.

Once I finally realized that, the switch flipped inside of me.

At the time, I didn't know this switch existed within me. I didn't know I had a choice. You have the same choice. Life is different when we wake up every day, excited about how we can give more. You, too, can flip the switch from getting to giving.

GOING FROM GETTING TO GIVING CHANGES EVERYTHING

I'm convinced something happens in heaven when we flip that switch.

Once I accepted that the purpose for my life was allowing God to use my hands to give more, God released something in heaven. I went from:

- Feeding my family to feeding thousands of families a month. This has continued for more than twenty years.
- Putting a roof over my family's head to being used by God to put roofs over the heads of hundreds of people.
- Going on solo mission trips to India to taking a thousand people there also.
- Planting one church to helping hundreds of pastors start their churches.
- Depending on income from the church to giving more to the church than I used to make.
- Turning one car back over to the bank to giving away more than twenty-five cars in three years.

- Losing our house to foreclosure to building houses for other families.
- From giving 10 percent tithe to the church and living on 90 percent to giving away more in one year than my whole annual salary the year before.

I could keep going. I am not trying to brag here, either. I am boasting about Almighty God.

Shelly and I have used the same tax preparer, Ed, for more than twenty-five years. He is a Christ-follower, meticulously thorough, and used to teach tax preparation for a local college. Thank God he knows ministers' tax inside and out. Each year, he prepares tax returns for many ministers, and very few have ever been audited by the IRS. He has guided Shelly and me in organizing our accounting and recordkeeping.

For the past ten years, I have served as the founder and executive director of Global Hope India. Our board of directors sets my salary. Ed will tell you my annual salary has not increased more than 3 percent per year over the past fifteen years. At the same time, our giving has increased more than 400 percent over the same time period. Although that is an indication of how little we used to give, it also indicates that God has enabled us to now give beyond a 10 percent tithe.

In 2015, Shelly and I were audited by the IRS. They

couldn't understand how we lived on so little and gave away so much. We provided copies of the receipts, and it was quickly settled. I could only agree that we showed a "higher than normal" percentage of our income as charitable contributions.

I actually have a hard time sharing with you about our giving. This is a personal and private matter between God, Shelly, and me. I don't share this to impress you. I'm only sharing this with you to be a witness for Christ and give an example of audacious generosity. You need to see audacious generosity is possible. It's real. If it can happen through me, it can certainly happen through you.

I know Shelly and I are not alone. There are many Believers who outgive us by miles. I hope you do. I want you to run circles around us. God is able to do so much more than what we've allowed Him to do through us.

There is freedom in accepting we are stewards, not proprietors. Something happens in heaven when we commit to let God give through us. We begin to experience, receive, and give more than we ever thought possible. God is waiting to cast you in the stories of His miracles, but you have to flip that switch from getting more to giving more. You can do it!

THE JOY OF GIVING AWAY ONE MILLION DOLLARS

Jesus promises it is more blessed to give than to receive. We've already talked about the joy we would get in giving away one million dollars, even if it were someone else's money. Consider how fulfilling and meaningful it would be to give away that amount of money and the lives you could forever change. Waking up every day to that purpose would be awesome.

This is the picture of audacious generosity. This is what it looks like to be one of God's stewards here on earth.

I'm going to invest a great deal of time in this chapter sharing with you what God has taught me about stewarding His resources from heaven onto earth. I am convinced the key to audacious generosity is found in spending time with God and getting to know what He values. There is no quick and instant download here. What I'm about to share has taken me more than twenty years to learn—and I'm still learning! God's ways are so much higher than ours. We have to make major adjustments to conform to His ways.

Allow me to share twelve things God values as revealed in His Word.

1: GOD VALUES STEWARDSHIP

By stewardship, I mean we understand that God owns

everything we have. Every time Shelly and I receive income, we return the first 10 percent or a tithe back to God. There is no shortage of Scriptures on this subject: Gen. 14:19–20, Gen. 28:20–22, Lev. 27:30–34, Num. 18:21, Num. 18:26, Deut. 12:5–6, Deut. 14:22, Deut. 14:28–29, 2 Chron. 31:4–5, Neh. 10:35–37, Prov. 3:9–10, Amos 4:4–5, Mal. 3:8–9, Mal. 3:10–12, Matt. 6:1–4, Matt. 23:23, Mark 12:41–44, Luke 11:42, Luke 18:9–14, Heb. 7:1–2.

We remember from where it comes. We are stewards of the remaining 90 percent. God is the owner of it all. We live openhandedly assured of our security in Christ and grateful to be a channel by which God flows His resources from heaven onto the earth. We share. We manage. That's why financial management is so important. It's that simple. That's stewardship.

2: GOD VALUES FIRST FRUITS

God used *The Blessed Life* series by Pastor Robert Morris of Gateway Church in Dallas, Texas to teach us the principle of "First Fruits" (Leviticus 23:10, Exodus 22:29, 1 Corinthians 15:20-23). When Jesus says, "You will know the truth and the truth will set you free" (John 8:32) (NIV), He was not kidding. I struggled my whole life to give a tithe only to learn we can't give a tithe to God. All we can do is return the tithe back to God. It's not ours to give. This was the beginning of my journey from getting to giving.

3: GOD VALUES BLESSING YOU

Shelly and I immediately began to systematically return a 10 percent tithe back to God (Malachi 3:8). God used Pastor Robert to make it clear: we can either live under a curse or a blessing. Right then and there, Shelly and I decided we would be more than glad to live on the remaining 90 percent. Since then, we have not missed returning the full tithe to God. This unlocked the door to God's blessings in our life.

We can't rob God of our tithes and offerings and expect to live a life of audacious generosity.

That would be like your friend stealing your car and then coming to ask you for a ride—it would be ridiculous.

4: GOD VALUES OBEDIENCE

It takes courage and freedom to simply obey. No matter your convictions, I encourage you to always err on the side of faith and obedience (Luke 6:46). Jesus is worth it. God is always faithful. We can never outgive God. Audacious generosity has to do with way more than just our financial giving.

5: GOD VALUES HIS WHY FOR GIVING

God only offers us two reasons to give. The first: God's more is more *of* Himself. The second: God's more is more *for* Himself. The same is true through you. We are to give everything we give to result in more *of* God or more *for* God (1 Corinthians 10:23-33). Adopting God's motives for giving changes everything. It is important that you understand God is only interested in you giving more *of* Him to others or more *for* Him to others. When I accepted the purpose of my giving is for more *of* God or more *for* God, something released in heaven. It's like the floodgates opened up.

6: GOD VALUES ETERNAL LIFE

In John 3:16, we see the reason God loved the whole world and gave Jesus is so that people would not perish, but have eternal life. God's motives for giving will always lead you to His compassion for the lost, His desire for the gospel to be advanced, and for the Great Commission to be fulfilled.

7: GOD VALUES COMPASSION FOR THOSE FACING A CHRISTLESS ETERNITY

Eternity is at stake in the lives of billions of people far from God. The Bible teaches us there are two options (Romans 6:23). Everyone on the planet will either spend eternity in Option A: Heaven in the presence of God, or in Option B: Hell outside the presence of God. There is no Option C.

8: GOD VALUES THE GREAT COMMISSION

I encourage you to see how God is setting the stage for your life to be a miracle. Audacious generosity is God's strategy for fulfilling the Great Commission. Fulfilling the Great Commission requires a miracle just like the Feeding of the Multitude did in John 6:5-15. Just like then, God is looking for empty hands He can fill for His mission.

9: GOD VALUES THE ADVANCEMENT OF THE GOSPEL

The main reason for audacious generosity is for the advancement of the gospel. Consider the three billion people alive today that have no access to the gospel. Their need for salvation is no different than the need for food during the miracle of the Feeding of the Multitude.

10: GOD VALUES AUDACIOUS GENEROSITY

In the Feeding of the Multitude, the disciples experienced, received, and gave more than they ever thought possible. They literally took the pieces of fish and loaves, which Jesus had just broken and blessed, and began distributing it to the people. What man produced (a small boy's lunch) was multiplied by what God could produce.

11: GOD VALUES MIRACLES

Depending on what we can produce is like putting out the flames of hell with a medicine dropper one drop at a time. Depending on what God can produce is like putting out the flames of hell with a forceful firehose that never runs dry. We can give the proportion that we can produce (tiny) or we can give the proportion of what God can produce (limitless). Our proportion is like, "So what?" God's proportion brings heaven to earth.

12: GOD VALUES MULTIPLICATION

We don't need addition. We need multiplication. I want you to keep hearing God say, "You can feed your family, but I can feed the multitude."

Flipping the switch from getting more to giving more is important because the watching world needs to see the miracles only God can perform. When it comes to accumulating more, it seems a lot of us flip the verse Mark 8:36, "What good is it for someone to gain the whole world, yet forfeit their soul?" (NIV). We say, "Oh, heaven forbid that anyone lose their soul." We take Jesus only for salvation and say, "check," thinking we are now allowed to gain the whole world. Accumulate more. Rent more storage units. Buy more. This is an indication of having a wrong perspective of God's more, His motives, and His strategy.

THE VALUE OF A HUMAN SOUL

What is the value of a human soul? Nothing is worth anyone spending eternity separated from God in hell because I got more instead of giving more.

Now, I am not anti-material possession. Our family owns a home. We have dependable cars. I own multiple modest-priced shoes, watches, and wallets from multiple countries around the world. God has not stripped our family of material possessions. That's not the point. The point is that our purpose is not rooted in seeking more. Instead, our focus is on giving more, more, and more.

Jesus promises that it is more blessed to give than to receive. It has been well said that we are most like Jesus when we are giving. We can't outgive God. Since flipping the switch from getting more to giving more, I have experienced, received, and given more than I ever thought possible. I am not perfect. I can be selfish and greedy, but my purpose drives me back to audacious generosity—and that's when miraculous things occur. Look at Matthew 7:11, "So if you sinful people know how to give good gifts to your children, how much more will your heavenly Father give good gifts to those who ask Him," (NLT).

The more I give, the more I get. I'm not giving to get. I am giving to give, but then I turn around and see that I have always received. When I say,

> "God's more is never a subtraction of His blessings to you. God's more is always a multiplication of His blessings to others through you,"

I mean it. I've lived it. It is my personal experience backed up by the Word of God.

RAISE YOUR STANDARD OF GIVING

In college, I was challenged by the story of John Wesley. I had just begun to experience a living relationship with God the year before. I was undisciplined in giving 2 percent of my income, much less tithing 10 percent.

By the end of his life, John Wesley was known for living on 10 percent of his income and giving 90 percent of his income. Wesley lived in the 1700s and was greatly impacted by an event that occurred while he was a student at Oxford. After purchasing some pictures for his room on a cold winter day, he noticed that one of the housekeepers had nothing to protect herself from the cold except a thin garment. When he reached into his pocket to give her some money to buy a coat, he found he didn't have enough left to pay for a coat. Immediately, he thought how God was not pleased with the way he had spent his money. He asked himself, "Will my Master say, 'Well done, good and faithful steward?' You have adorned your walls with the money which might have protected this poor woman from the cold.

O justice. O mercy. Are not these pictures the blood of this poor maid?"

From that day on, Wesley determined to maintain his standard of living at the same level and give away everything above that threshold. At that time, with earnings of 30 pounds and living expenses at 28 pounds, he gave away two pounds. When his earnings increased to 60 pounds, he gave away 32. As they increased to 120 pounds, he continued to live on 28 and give away 92 pounds. Wesley became known for his saying: "What should rise is not the Christian's standard of living, but his standard of giving."

He continued this practice his entire life. Even when his income reached 1,400 pounds, he lived on 30 pounds and gave the rest away. Because Wesley had a fear of laying up treasures on earth, the money went out in charity as quickly as it came in. He reports that he never had 100 pounds at any one time.

When I heard about John Wesley's life, that level of giving was so foreign to me. You might as well have said John Wesley was one of the angels in heaven. I couldn't comprehend how that could happen on earth. I'm sure you've heard similar stories. These stories can be very convicting. I remember feeling frustrated because the story didn't include a "how to" manual. That's why I am determined for this book to be a very practical "how to" guide.

DECIDING IN ADVANCE

Audacious generosity is about determining in ADVANCE what you are going to do with what God puts into your hands. Luke 14:28-30 provides the principle of budgeting and planning. If you're feeling some tension here, I encourage you to consider going through Dave Ramsey's Financial Peace University.

As God has given me the opportunity of audacious generosity, He has led me to:

1. Return the full 10 percent tithe to Him.
2. Set up a spending account for my wife. Her sense of security is second to our tithe.
3. Cap what I need to take care of my family.
4. Commit in advance to give away any surplus.

MOTIVES MATTER

Nothing gets in the way of generosity like our motives do. James 4:3 offers a very sobering warning about having pure motives. Let God replace your motives with His motives. This warning in James should be heard in the context of Psalm 37:4, Matthew 6:33, and Philippians 4:19.

The opposite of James 4:3 is also true. James is also offering a bold promise that when you ask God with pure motives to bring Him glory, you should expect to receive what you ask.

I am convinced God is incredibly honored when we hold Him to His Word. With all this, we should always remember how Jesus taught us to pray, "Father, not my will, but yours be done," like we read in Luke 22:42. This is about trusting God, not bossing Him around.

FLIP THE SWITCH

By flipping the switch from getting more to giving more, you have nothing to lose and everything to gain.

The more Believers living with audacious generosity, the quicker the Great Commission is fulfilled.

Nothing brings more fulfillment than knowing you are experiencing God as you join Him in His mission.

Allowing God to give more through you according to His values enables you to freely give to others what God puts into your hands. The only thing that could hold you back is not committing in advance to freely give to others what God puts into your hands.

GIVING AWAY SO MUCH MORE THAN A MILLION DOLLARS

God is offering you the opportunity to give away way more than one million dollars. His only stipulation is that you get to know Him and understand His values. He promises to take care of you, which frees you to focus on His mission. He wants you to use what He places into your hands to further His mission. Look how fulfilling and meaningful it would be to give away God's gifts. Your life would have so much purpose as God uses you to bring heaven to earth.

The third step toward audacious generosity is setting others free. Living generously for God allows you to give more than you ever thought possible. We need to set others free so that our world matches God's world as seen in John 3:16. Congratulations on flipping the switch from getting more to giving more.

In the next chapter, we'll explore flipping the switch from greed to generosity.

CHAPTER 13

GREED OR GENEROSITY?

We are physically born into a fallen and greedy world. Greed is a noun meaning intense and selfish desire for something, especially wealth, power, or food. It has been well said that sin is a three-letter word with "I" right in the middle of it. No one has to teach us to be motivated by greed. Because of the sin of Adam and Eve, we are programmed for greed.

As soon as we take Jesus only for salvation, we are filled with the Holy Spirit and given another choice: generosity. Generosity is a noun meaning the quality of being kind and plentiful. After salvation, generosity is now within us. In Galatians 5, Paul gives us a great explanation of what it looks like to walk in step with the Spirit. On a practical level, we have a choice. We can continue to be controlled and motivated by greed *or* we can yield to the Generous One within us and allow generosity to control and motivate us.

Greed versus generosity thus represents the second switch on our way to setting others free. My advice is to flip this switch as soon as possible, put a lockbox over it, and then throw away the key.

HOW MUCH GREED IS OK?

Perhaps you've seen the AT&T commercials themed around the saying, "Just okay is not okay." One of the commercials shows a nervous surgeon who was just reinstated, asking his patient if he was nervous about going into surgery. The patient has a look of fear across his face. The surgeon says, "Me too. Don't worry. We will figure it out," as he walks out of the room. The announcer says, "Just okay is not okay." Then you hear the message of the reliability of AT&T.

How much greed is acceptable? No amount of greed is okay. That question is like asking how much cancer is acceptable. How much water is acceptable in your gas tank? How much dirt is acceptable in your food? The answer is none.

LOOKING GREED IN THE FACE

I remember the day I looked greed in the face.

While the miracle food was being poured out on us, the financial hardships continued. One day, I drove our minivan back over to the bank and handed the bank manager, Mike, the keys. Mike and I were on a first-name basis.

It didn't stop with our car. Three times over a year-and-a-half, we faced foreclosure on our home. The first two times God miraculously bailed us out in the midnight hour. The third time I prayed, "Father, take the house." This prayer represented a place of surrender. I was finally surrendering the house only I could produce in exchange for the house(s) only God can produce.

The mortgage was foreclosed. We'd never been through anything like this. Here we were, distributing food every day to hundreds of families per month. The fruit of ministry was happening all around us. The transformation we had earlier worked so hard to achieve was now happening right in front of us. Again, it was a mix of gore and glory. We were doing God's work, but no one was handing us a paycheck. It didn't matter, though, because we were free. We had a sense God was going to make everything right in that house, but we were wrong.

God never led us to move out. We packed a week's worth of clothes for each of our family of six and put it into the trunk of the car. One day, after delivering food to the needy, we returned home and found signs from the Sheriff's department that we had been evicted from the house. The locks had been changed. We were not allowed to enter.

I kept waiting for the bank manager to call me with good news. He never did. One day, we drove down the hill to collect our mail and there was a box truck from a local charity removing all our earthly belongings. Shelly started kicking the floorboard of the car screaming, "They are taking our baby pictures!" To say we were distraught is an understatement.

The bank manager was there. Within seconds we were all crying together. "Why didn't you move out?" Mike asked. "What are you doing with our stuff?" I responded. And just like that, our minivan, house, and earthly possessions were gone. All we had was a week's worth of clothes and a used car someone had given to us.

Within seconds, God intervened as Mike asked the movers to stop removing anymore from the house. Mike said to me, "If you move out today, you can have what still remains in the house." Neighbors from all sides were standing in the front yard asking how they could help. I asked the movers from the charity about our belongings they had already removed. They told us to go to the charity to speak to the director about buying back our belongings. I had no money, but God intervened as several neighbors opened their wallets and started handing cash to me saying, "Go get your stuff." Within thirty minutes, neighbors and friends from church had arranged another truck. They began moving four bedrooms and 2,500 square feet worth of furniture out of the house and putting it into storage.

While our neighbors helped pack our belongings, Shelly and I drove to the charity's warehouse where our belongings were taken. The movers from the charity had come in and grabbed the most valuable items first—electronics, bikes, Shelly's wedding band, etc. I approached the director and asked her for our valuables back. "I have to pay my workers, so you can buy it all back for $400." I handed her $400 from the generosity of our neighbors and started pulling our possessions out into a pile. Our belongings were scattered throughout the warehouse, which was ginormous. The director took the money and left, leaving us to deal with her staff, who didn't want to give back our belongings. That didn't stop us, though. We kept finding more and refusing to take no for an answer. We eventually found and took back 95 percent of our belongings.

It was a hot summer day. I waited outside the warehouse with the pile of our belongings for a neighbor to bring a box truck. I reflected on what was happening. While God had set me free in Christ, I was still confused. "Why is this happening?" I asked God. I had been praying. I wasn't rebelling. I had been seeking to know and do God's will. God impressed upon me, "I needed you to see greed. I want you to despise it as I do. Have nothing to do with it. Weep over it as I do."

All day long, my heart had been breaking. Instead of helping us in our time of need, the charity took advantage of our misfortune. This was one of the first times in my life I experienced the exploitation of the poor. In that moment, I was the person I was to now go and serve. In Matthew 9:36, we read, "When Jesus saw the crowds, he had compassion on them, because they were harassed and helpless, like sheep without a shepherd," (NIV). God was breaking my heart for billions of hurting people around the world forced to suffer lives of financial and spiritual poverty because of greed.

That day under that shade tree, I looked greed in the face. That's when With Love from Jesus Ministries was born.

Three months later, without any money in our hands, God moved us into a 3,000 square-foot house on a half-acre lot. God intervened as eight churches put up the funds, and one local pastor co-signed the lease in order for our family to have a home. This house had a full basement with a roll-up door that opened up to a large parking area. People started asking us if they could give us their gently used clothes to share with the families we were serving. Within one month, the basement was full of clothes. One Saturday, a group of volunteers helped pull everything out. It looked like a gigantic yard sale without price tags. We gave it all away free with love from Jesus. Several people insisted on paying, but we refused. People were just dumbfounded by the generosity and love. We had the opportunity to pray with hundreds of people. The fruit of ministry was occurring all around us.

A month later, it happened again. Then again two weeks later. Within a few months, we were in a 5,000 square-foot warehouse. God intervened through a local family who took me to lunch and gave me a check for $11,000 for WLFJ and another check for $5,000 for Shelly and me. It was the most money I had seen in years. We used the gift for WLFJ toward the lease on the warehouse space. We used the gift for us to pay cash on a used minivan for our family. God had begun to transition us from what we could produce to what He could produce. We were totally free to focus on the needs of others.

When we moved into the warehouse, I remember thinking we needed a sign to help people know where to enter. We made a sign that said, "With Love from Jesus."

That's how the With Love from Jesus Ministry in Raleigh, North Carolin was born in 2001. The following year, we moved into a 70,000 square-foot warehouse even closer to one of the poorest areas in our city. God intervened by leading a multibillion-dollar property development company to allow us to use this vacant strip mall space month-to-month for pennies on the dollar while they redeveloped the property. This was as miraculous as God parting the Red Sea (Exodus 14). This represented God winning a spiritual battle like when the Walls of Jericho fell down (Joshua 6). It wasn't easy to face the impossible. Each time God turned the impossible into possible. That was nearly twenty years ago. With Love from Jesus Ministries is still in a smaller portion of that strip mall today.

What started out as distributing food to the poor became clothing, furniture, appliances, household items, electronics, and even automobiles. The more we gave away, the more we received. God intervened through endless donations from families and businesses as the word got out around the community.

As families in need arrived, we shared a passage of Scripture with them and offered to pray with them before they shopped. Everything was free "With Love from Jesus." We saw hundreds of people come to faith in Christ, be healed, connected to a local church, and transformed as God revealed Himself in the midst of human need.

We were riding a wave of the Holy Spirit. I served at With Love from Jesus for seven years and turned it over to the leadership God had raised up. The miracle of WLFJ still continues. Every year for more than twenty years, God has used hundreds of Believers from over fifty churches to distribute millions of dollars in resources to high-need populations and see thousands of lives transformed by the gospel.

God knows no greed.

THE ATTRACTION OF GENEROSITY

I don't think I have to convince you of the value of generosity. The value of generosity is to experience God. If experiencing God wasn't important, you wouldn't be with me on this journey.

I am convinced audacious generosity is a manifestation of the presence of God within us. That manifestation influences and controls every aspect of our life.

Audacious generosity is our identity given by God. It is our witness of Christ to a watching world. Audacious generosity is not a thing that we do. Nothing sets back the gospel more than greed in one of Jesus' followers. There is no greater contradiction to the cross of Jesus Christ than for one of Jesus' followers to be greedy, self-centered, and inhospitable.

We all know the joy and pleasure of benefitting from people with generous hospitality. Don't you just love to be in someone's home who can't stop bringing you more to drink and eat? The food is always so good. The conversation is easy and filled with blessing. The atmosphere overflows with joy. Yes, indeed, it is great to be served with kindness and plenty.

The opposite is also true. We all know the horror of being in the home of a family void of generous hospitality. Isn't it challenging to be in someone's home where you have to ask for a glass of water because your mouth is dry? Ever been served stale snacks? Made to feel like you were more of a burden? The conversation feels like a root canal. The atmosphere is thick with dread. You just can't wait to leave.

Why would we expect people far from God to want to be a part of our family of God if we are greedy, self-centered, and inhospitable?

> There is nothing more attractive for the Gospel than audacious generosity.

For more than twenty years in India, I've witnessed the power of generosity firsthand. God has led Global Hope India to do one thing in India, and that is to make Christ known among people with limited access to hear about Jesus. We do everything we do through the local church in India in order to advance the gospel. Our ministry model consists of three pillars: (1) Pray (2) Give, and (3) Go. We call people to stand in the gap through prayer, give financially to empower the church in India, and to go or send people on short-term mission trips to India. When it comes to fulfilling the Great Commission, the Bible only gives us three options: (1) Go (2) Send, or (3) be disobedient. This is how we see results of expanding heaven and fulfilling the Great Commission.

We take a variety of teams over to serve the church in India and empower them in their outreach of the gospel. All the travelers from the USA raise their own support. We always seek to be a blessing and never a burden to the church we are serving. Whether it is a medical team, children's program team, or construction team, all the programs we do are completely free. Over and over, I have witnessed how God uses generosity to open the doors that were previously locked shut to the gospel.

There is nothing more attractive for the Gospel than audacious generosity.

One evidence of audacious generosity is unconditional love. God's love is unconditional. God has taught us so much about unconditional love. John 3:16 says, "For God so loved the world that He gave." Reject Him, and He still loves. Love Him in return, and He still loves. He has taught our teams to show the same unconditional love.

Unconditional means no conditions. Zero. Here's what we've learned:

1. Unconditional love means no strings attached.
2. Unconditional love does not manipulate.
3. Unconditional love does not control.
4. Unconditional love does not discriminate.
5. Unconditional love expects nothing in return.
6. Unconditional love leaves the results up to God.

7. Unconditional love honors God as The Giver.

Audacious generosity is shown through unconditional love. If someone rejects our unconditional love and generosity, they are rejecting God. They are not rejecting us. We don't have to be offended. We don't have to become defensive. God has truly set us free to give unconditionally.

> There is nothing more attractive for the Gospel than unconditional love.

We see the multiplication of the gospel. We see progress toward fulfilling the Great Commission.

One of my favorite quotes that reflects unconditional love is from John Bunyan, who said, "You have not lived today until you have done something for someone who can never repay you." This is audacious generosity in its purest form.

CHANGING THE GENEROSITY CULTURE

Just out of curiosity, I did some research on the current culture of generosity. I came across five credible sources that opened my eyes. The first is from Push Pay Research. In their 2019 Church Giving Report, they found:

1. **Consistent givers only make up 10-25 percent of the church.** Research points to the 80/20 factor, where

80 percent of giving is done by only 20 percent of the people.

2. **Eight out of ten consistent givers have zero credit card debt.** For many, credit card debt is a barrier to giving.

3. **Giving to missions is down 50 percent since 1990.** Additional sources state 99 percent is spent on sharing the gospel with people who already have access to the gospel. Only 1 percent is used to share the gospel with people without access to the gospel.

4. **On Average, Christians give only 2.5 percent of their income to churches.**

5. **Of families that make $75,000+, only 1 percent donated a tenth of their income.** Most people tend to think, "If I make more, I will give more." Research shows otherwise.

6. **Of ALL the giving done, only a third goes to religious organizations.** This means two-thirds of all giving isn't for the purpose of more of God or more for God.

7. **People who attend church give more than those who don't.**

8. **Recurring givers annually donate 42 percent more than one-time donors.** Generosity is a lifestyle, not a one-time occurrence.

Imagine how much faster the Great Commission could be fulfilled if every Believer joined God's movement of audacious generosity.

The second point of research I came across was from LifeWay Research. LifeWay asked pastors how often they preach on financial giving. A fifth of all pastors say they have never preached on tithing.

I found The Generosity Project by the Evangelical Council for Financial Accountability (ECFA) especially interesting in identifying the mindset of how people give. Baby boomers had a tendency to give monetarily. Millennials give by donating their time.

In 2017, ECFA released a study that analyzed the giving patterns of the largest generation, millennials. The Generosity Project uncovered a pattern of optimism among young donors, who cite feeling hopeful and satisfied after giving. Millennials indicate being highly engaged and invested with the ministries and organizations they support financially.

Here's what the ECFA survey learned about generosity:

1. Most people believe the Bible commands them to give. They have differing views about what it means to tithe.
2. Millennials (born between 1980 and 1994) are twice as likely to feel generous as boomers (1944 and 1964). Boomers give more but feel less satisfied about their giving. Millennials give less but feel two times more satisfied than boomers.

3. Millennials are more inclined to give because of who they are, while older generations are more inclined to give because of which ministry asked them to give.
4. Millennials will give you more money if you encourage them to make a "meaningful" gift rather than a "generous" one. Meaningful means useful quality or purpose. Generous means willingness to give more of something.
5. Fifty-six percent of the 16,500 Christians surveyed said they gave less than $50 to church and charity last year. Eighty-four percent of the millennials surveyed reported that they gave less than $50 dollars to church and charity last year. Seventy-eight percent of those millennials said they were satisfied with their level of giving.
6. Thirty-two percent of Christians strongly associated generosity with service or volunteering, 30 percent with emotional or relational support, 22 percent with giving money, 12 percent with hospitality, and 5 percent with nonmonetary gifts. Only 13 percent of millennials associate generosity with monetary giving.

The Generosity Gap by Barna Group illustrates that what people say and what they do are not the same when it comes to generosity. We all say we love generosity, but our actions don't reflect that. This study proves that.

In 2017, Thrivent Financial collaborated with the Barna Group in a groundbreaking study of generosity among

Christians. The Barna Group found significant gaps in understandings, expectations, and practices within the US Christian community about giving.

Among the study's key findings:

1. Ninety-six percent of Christians surveyed said generosity is important to them.
2. Sixteen percent said they are most often generous to others through monetary support.
3. Forty-seven percent of Christians surveyed agreed that it is okay for church members who volunteer extensively not to give financially.

Christopher Kopka, president of Thrivent Church Solutions Group, said, "Generosity is both a reflection of people's heart and a reflection of their wisdom with money." David Kinnaman, president of Barna Group, said, "The challenge is to create moments that invite extravagant generosity from people as they serve an extravagantly generous Lord." I couldn't agree more.

What we say about being generous and what we do about being generous is not consistent. When it comes to the research about generosity, the numbers prove that our actions speak louder than words.

The Science of Generosity research program at The University of Notre Dame stated: "Americans pride themselves on being generous. Two-thirds of Americans believe it's important to be generous. Yet, almost half of the US population actually gave no money to charity at all."

The Science of Generosity research program evolved out of Christian Smith's work on *Passing the Plate: Why American Christians Don't Give Away More Money.** That book examines the complex reasons for the illiberal financial giving of American Christians. The research clearly showed that more liberal giving could accomplish world-transforming change. I agree. More people need to flip the switch to generosity.

In Malachi 3:10, God says, "Bring all the tithes into the storehouse so there will be enough food in my Temple. If you do," says the LORD of Heaven's Armies, "I will open the windows of heaven for you. I will pour out a blessing so great you won't have enough room to take it in. Try it. Put me to the test," (NLT).

Look at Luke 6:38. Jesus says, "Give, and you will receive. Your gift will return to you in full—pressed down, shaken together to make room for more, running over, and poured

---

* Smith, Christian and Michael Emerson with Patricia Snell. *Passing the Plate: Why American Christians Don't Give Away More Money.* New York: Oxford University Press, 2008.

into your lap. The amount you give will determine the amount you get back," (NLT).

Flipping the switch between greed and generosity results in opening the floodgates of heaven. If God's promises are true, why would we ever want to walk the path of greed?

The third step toward audacious generosity is setting others free. Living generously for God allows you to give more than you ever thought possible. Congratulations on flipping the switch from greed to generosity.

In the next chapter, we'll discuss flipping the switch from burden to blessing.

It is time to see others as a blessing.

CHAPTER 14

BURDEN OR BLESSING?

Until audacious generosity includes everyone, it can't be possible.

I wish someone would have sat me down and told me about the switch between burden or blessing. I wish someone would have said, "Save yourself a ton of grief and flip the switch from burden to blessing."

I personally believe as soon as you flip the switch, things start changing.

Until the availability of your generosity equals the availability of God's generosity, it will never be audacious generosity.

John 3:16 says, "For God so loved the world." It could have said, "For God so loved the Jews," "For God so loved men," "For God so loved the English," "...the fair-skinned," "...the poor," "...the straight," "...the educated," "...the people who shop at Target."

Every person has a name, a soul, and a value to God. He made us all. John 3:16 includes everyone. No one is exempt.

LET'S FACE IT; WE ARE JUDGMENTAL

Which of the seven billion people on planet Earth would be a burden to you if God wanted to use you to be generous to them? Which one of these people would you not want to stand beside? Which one of these people would you not want to serve? Murderers? Rapists? Terrorists? Asians? Blacks? Whites? Mexicans? Pentecostals? Republicans? Democrats? Homeless? Addicts? Child Molesters?

I'm not asking you to agree or disagree.

I'm not asking you to approve of having been victimized.

I'm not asking what acts you consider to be unforgivable.

No matter who they are or what they've done, whether they have done something to you or someone else, God calls us to love them. To accept them. The reality is Jesus died for everyone. The rapist. The child molester. The terrorist. Jesus died for all of them. Otherwise, He wouldn't have died for me. Otherwise, He wouldn't have died for you.

LET'S FACE IT; WE SEE PEOPLE AS BAD

My whole life I've been told that unplanned pregnancies are bad. Illegal immigrants are bad. Prisoners are bad. Drug addicts are bad. Many consider Hollywood bad. Many consider being married bad. Christians are bad. Politicians are bad. Start filtering what you see and hear through this filter of burden or blessing, and you'll see how we are influenced to see people as a burden.

LET'S FACE IT; WE DISCRIMINATE

Our world discriminates against people who have a different skin color, nationality, sexual practice, faith, creed, body shape, age, gender, language, financial status, educational level, political party, lifestyle, and religion. No human being is fully free of prejudice or discrimination. It's part of our selfish nature to prefer those of our own kind, whatever that represents to us. The goal should be to disagree without discriminating. There should be no discrimination within the Body of Christ because there is no discrimination with God (Acts 10:34).

LET'S FACE IT; WE ARE QUICK TO BLAME

There are some classic examples:

Blaming the poor people for being poor.

Blaming the homeless for being homeless.

Blaming higher taxes on illegal immigrants.

Blaming overweight people for being overweight.

Blaming the government for mass shootings.

Blaming the media for fostering fear.

Blaming your boss for being fired.

It is always someone else's fault.

LET'S FACE IT; WE SEE PEOPLE AS AN ENEMY

Have you ever been hurt? Ever had enemies? I have.

Several years ago, I returned from a summer of fruitful ministry in India to learn that five people from the first team of the summer had returned and written letters to our board of directors asking for my removal. This hurt me. None of these brothers and sisters in Christ had ever spoken one word to me about their concerns. I had worked hard to serve them without them knowing of a medical condition I was dealing with during their trip. I had taken them on a mission trip to India only for them to make it their mission to take me out as the leader.

Unfortunately, there was no biblical order of following Matthew 18. They went to our board, filed their complaints, asked for my removal, and said, "We do not want him to contact us." Fortunately, the board of directors handled the situation with grace and truth. Still, I was hurt that my own brothers and sisters in Christ could do this to me.

All of a sudden, the Holy Spirit led me to John 17 and broke my heart through Jesus' prayer for The Church to be protected. For weeks, I camped out in John 17 and kept seeing how Jesus prayed for: (1) our protection; (2) that we'd be set apart for His glory; and (3) for our unity. Just like that, I no longer cared what had been said against me. It was obvious that God had used spiritual warfare to birth a new work in my heart. I began to see that John 17 is the Lord's Prayer I'd never prayed before. From that time forward, our staff and board of directors now prays John 17 constantly over Global Hope India and the church around the world.

The first thing God taught me was to start praying for others the way Jesus does in John 17.

The second thing God taught me was to decide in advance that people are never the enemy. My whole life, I've heard that we as Believers worship an audience of one, which is God. Throughout Scripture, Satan is identified as the enemy. Determining that there is one audience (God) and one enemy (Satan) has resulted in so much freedom in my life. I no longer see people as the enemy. I don't see people as a burden. The temptation has been diffused. God is in control. I rest in that. Until you rule out the possibility of people becoming your enemy, you'll not know the audacious generosity portrayed by Jesus.

The third thing God taught me was to always protect my brothers and sisters in Christ. God showed me that I can only control myself. I am determined to always protect my brothers and sisters. I will have nothing to do with talking badly about any brother or sister in Christ. I am not afraid to address conflict with truth and grace, but I will not gossip. I will not bear a false witness. I do not have to agree with you to protect you. I've done many things Jesus didn't agree with, and He always protected me. The same is true of you too.

I encourage you to extend to all people the same protection God gives you. Doing so will enable you to experience God's audacious generosity through you.

Audacious generosity is not judgmental. Audacious generosity doesn't discriminate. Audacious generosity blesses everyone. Audacious generosity frees everyone from being seen as a burden.

You can't hate some people but be generous to others. That's not audacious generosity. You can't be racist and generous to some. That's not audacious generosity. You can't hurt some people but be generous to others. That's not audacious generosity.

Look at what Jesus says to us in Matthew 5:43-48, "You have heard the law that says, 'Love your neighbor' and hate your enemy. But I say, love your enemies. Pray for those who persecute you. In that way, you will be acting as true children of your Father in heaven. For He gives His sunlight to both the evil and the good, and He sends rain on the just and the unjust alike. If you love only those who love you, what reward is there for that? Even corrupt tax collectors do that much. If you are kind only to your friends, how are you different from anyone else? Even pagans do that. But you are to be perfect, even as your Father in heaven is perfect," (NLT). Wow. Now, that makes it very clear.

God's been teaching me a lot about unconditional love and unconditional gratitude. Jesus died for those who worship Him as well as those who mock Him. The gospel is for all. We are to love all and serve all.

We are human. We get scared. Fear is the driving force behind racism, prejudice, and discrimination. It requires a lot of courage to set others free. God makes all the courage we need available for us to take. The reason we take the courage to set others free is for audacious generosity.

I encourage you not to allow any obstacle to stand in the way of setting God, yourself, and others free. Nothing is worth you not experiencing, receiving, and giving more than you ever thought possible. Nothing.

WITH WHOM WILL YOU SHARE HEAVEN?

Revelation 7:9-12 gives us a picture of what heaven will look like as people of every tribe, tongue, and nation are worshipping Jesus before the throne. Is there anyone with whom you are unwilling to share heaven? God forbid we go to heaven and be shocked to see certain people there. Who will shock you to see in heaven? Prostitutes? Terrorists? People you thought were Muslims? Blacks? Whites? Homosexuals? Catholics? Conservatives? Liberals? Baptists? Cat owners?

There is only one qualification for admission into heaven and that is the blood of Jesus. God offers Jesus only for salvation to the whole world—that's anyone and everyone.

We are not allowed to add even one single extra qualification to our admission of heaven or to our generosity.

God makes the choice, not us, where His audacious generosity through us reaches.

If we exclude anyone, then audacious generosity isn't possible. No exclusions allowed.

WHY DO I GET TO KNOW JESUS?

Can you see what's happening? When we flip the switch from burden to blessing, we transition the sense of burden. People are no longer the burden to us. Instead, God gives us a genuine burden for people to know Him. There is no greater way to bless people than to carry a burden for them to know God. The presence of God is the greatest need for all of us.

I want to give you one of the most tender examples of audacious generosity. Many nights I have laid in my bed weeping as I ask God over and over why I get to know Christ while a billion people in India are facing a Christless eternity? After more than fifty trips to India, it becomes pretty clear the primary difference between our life of comfort and their life of poverty is our place of birth. We did nothing to earn the blessed life we live in the USA. Why do we get to have access to the gospel and all the comforts of the world when they don't even yet know about Jesus? I'm not going to pretend to know everything about predestination and free will, but don't dare think you deserve what you got and they deserve what they got. I confess to you the only thing good in me is Jesus. The reason I lay in bed crying for those far from God is that I allow Jesus to cry through me. You should, too.

Matthew 9:35-38 says, "Jesus traveled through all the towns and villages of that area, teaching in the synagogues and announcing the Good News about the Kingdom. And He healed every kind of disease and illness. When He saw the crowds, He had compassion on them because they were confused and helpless, like sheep without a shepherd. He said to His disciples, "The harvest is great, but the workers are few. So pray to the Lord who is in charge of the harvest; ask Him to send more workers into His fields," (NLT).

FLIP THE SWITCH

When we are born, we are programmed to see others as a burden. When we are born again, we receive the power to flip the switch from burden to blessing. Determine to bless others. Until you do, you will face endless temptations to be burdened by people. Your generosity will be conditional. That's not audacious generosity.

The third step toward audacious generosity is setting others free. There is no greater form of it. Love unconditionally. Accept unconditionally. Treat equally. That's audacious generosity.

Now let's apply God's Word.

CHAPTER 15

APPLICATION

SET OTHERS FREE—LIVE GENEROUSLY TO GIVE MORE

Have you ever been unable to get something off your mind? I have thought about India a lot.

Let me paint you a picture of what my heart feels when it comes to India. As I pray for India, God fills me with more and more love for the people of India. With 1.3 billion people, India is one of the largest, neediest, and most unreached countries in the world.

India is 75 percent Hindu, 20 percent Muslim, and less than 5 percent Christian. I don't just see a statistic of 1.3 billion people. Rather, I see 1.3 billion boys, girls, men, and women God created, loves, and sent Jesus to die for. I see 1.3 billion souls facing a Christless eternity in hell unless they know Jesus.

If you have any tension with me saying that people far from God are facing a Christless eternity in hell, then I encourage you to read *Radical* by David Platt. He provides a thorough study of Scripture showing two undeniable realities: (1) people far from God are without excuse; and (2) the people of God have been given the mission to go and tell.

When it comes to considering the needs of others as more important than ourselves, India has been and is my other. The question of how will India know Jesus haunts me. It alarms me that every day, 25,000 people in India die without having heard the gospel. That's 9,125,000 a year! I lay awake at night and cry out to God for the salvation of India. I can't stop staring at India.

I've seen what happens when we flip the switch. I've seen what happens when we go from get to give, from greed to generosity, and from burden to blessing. These three switches hold the power to either block or fuel audacious generosity. I know what happens when we offer others the same freedom God has given to us. I've seen how living generously is attractive to people far from God. I've been staring at India for twenty years. I'm convinced as more Believers live out audacious generosity, we can see the Great Commission fulfilled.

HOW TO SET OTHERS FREE

Setting others free is the key to living generously. The key to setting others free is inside you. Here are three specific applications that will empower you to live generously and set others free.

APPLICATION #1: EXCHANGE YOUR NEEDS FOR THE NEEDS OF OTHERS

Open your journal to a new page. At the very top of the page, write the words, "God's Focus becomes My Focus." Now draw a straight line down the middle of your page. At the top of the left column, write, "My Needs." At the top of the right column, write, "The Needs of Others." In the "My Needs" column, list your top seven needs. Be practical. In "The Needs of Others" column, list the top seven needs of those who are currently far from God. You might start with: the presence of God, salvation, forgiveness of sin, someone to share the Gospel with them, and hope.

Notice the difference between the two columns. Write the word "Confident" at the top of your column. I want you to be confident that God knows your needs and has committed to supply all your needs according to His riches in Christ Jesus (Philippians 4:19). In "The Needs of Others" column, write the words, "God's Call—My Mission." Here and now I want you to respond, "Lord, Here Am I. Send Me" (Isaiah 6:8).

With the confidence that God will meet your needs, you are free to consider the needs of others. This allows you to make the needs of others first and foremost in your life. Take time to meditate on the verse in Philippians 2:3. Reflect on how God is moving within you right now. Let Him exchange the concern for yourself with the concern for others. Remember that eternity is at stake for billions of lost souls without access to the gospel. Let God transition your burden *by* people to a burden *for* people. God's strategy is audacious generosity through you.

Key Verse: Do nothing out of selfish ambition or vain conceit. Rather, in humility value others above yourselves (Philippians 2:3) (NIV).

The Point: We set others free when we live confident of God's care for us.

APPLICATION #2: EXCHANGE YOUR VALUES, MOTIVES, AND MISSION FOR GOD'S

Open to a new page in your journal. Draw a straight line down the middle, then evenly divide the page into three sections. At the top of section one, in the left column, write "My Values." In the right column, write "God's Values." At the top of section two in the left column, write "My Motives." In the right column, write "God's Motives." At the top of section three, in the left column write, "My Mission." Across the page, write "God's Mission."

In the "My Values" box, I want you to list your top three values. For example, this could be: the presence of God, my family, and my house. You decide. In the "God's Values" box, write the words to John 3:16. Circle what God values.

In the "My Motives" box, list your top three motives. This could be: to experience God, to be healthy, to be financially independent, or to be kind. You decide. In the "God's Motives" box, write the words to Luke 19:10. Circle what motivates God.

Finally, in the "My Mission" box, write your mission. This could include: to pursue God, to have a successful career, or to love your family well. In the "God's Mission" box, write the words to Matthew 28:18-20. Circle God's mission.

I want you to notice any differences between yours and God's. Across section one, write, "God's Values become My Values." I want you to pray and exchange your values for God's values. Surrender your values to God. Trust that He cares for you. Across section two, write, "God's Motives become My Motives." I want you to pray and exchange your motives for God's motives. Surrender your motives to God. Across section three, write, "God's Mission Becomes My

Mission." I want you to pray and exchange your mission for God's mission. Surrender your mission to God. Trust that He cares for you.

Take time to meditate on each of the Bible verses. Reflect on how God is moving within you right now. Let Him exchange your values, motives, and mission for His.

Key Verse: For this is how God loved the world: He gave His one and only Son, so that everyone who believes in Him will not perish but have eternal life (John 3:16) (NLT).

The Point: We set others free when we exchange our values, motives, and mission for God's.

APPLICATION #3: COMMIT IN ADVANCE TO GIVE AWAY ANY SURPLUS

In your journal, make a list of all budget categories for which you use your income to cover. I want you to pray and ask the Holy Spirit to guide you. For example: tithes and offerings, housing, utilities, medical, transportation, food, clothing, and grooming. Feel free to add more. I want you to take time and calculate your living cost. How much do you need? Does your current income cover what you need to cover your living cost? If not, then start praying specifically for God to cover this. He has promised to supply all your needs (Philippians 4:19).

If you already have surplus, then calculate the amount of surplus you have. I encourage you to honor God with your surplus and watch what He does in and through your life. Look at 2 Corinthians 9:7. God loves and honors planned giving. Prioritize God's values, motives, and mission above your own and watch what God does. Whether you have surplus right now or not, I encourage you to determine in advance that you are going to honor God with what He puts into your hands. I want you to agree that everything you are and have belongs to God. I want you to take a moment and open your hands before God. Pray and commit in advance to give away any surplus for the advancement of the gospel.

Watch what happens. I encourage you to take time to worship using the songs "Available" by Elevation Worship or "Follow You Anywhere" by Passion. There are many great humanitarian causes, but I want you to keep in mind that God's more is always more *of* Himself or more *for* Himself.

Keep in mind God's mission is to spread His presence upon the earth. Notice what Jesus says in Matthew 24:14, "This gospel of the kingdom will be preached in the whole world as a testimony to all nations, and then the end will come," (NIV). Invest God's surplus into the fulfillment of the Great Commission. Invest taking the gospel to people who are yet to hear about Jesus.

Key Verse: You must each decide in your heart how much

to give. And don't give reluctantly or in response to pressure. "For God loves a person who gives cheerfully (2 Corinthians 9:7) (NLT).

The Point: We set others free when we live openhandedly.

Taking these three action steps provides three benefits to you: living generously for God, setting others free to experience God's unconditional love and acceptance, and giving more of God than you ever thought possible.

CONGRATULATIONS ON SETTING OTHERS FREE

The result of you flipping the switch from get to give, from greed to generosity, and from burden to blessing is you setting others free. Setting others free allows you to live generously for God. Now nothing is limiting God from being the Giver and giving through you. Now God is free, you are free, and others are free. Now your motives and intentions align with God's motives and intentions. Now you can wake up every day looking for ways to be more generous. This is the life God has always wanted for you. This is the life you have always wanted.

PASTOR RAJA OPENS HIS HANDS AND HIS HOME

One year after I returned from my first trip to India, I received a letter from Pastor Raja, a local pastor in Hyderabad, India, which took a month to arrive by boat. In the letter, Pastor Raja said, "I can no longer align myself with the Lord Jesus Christ and ignore the cries of the poor on my doorstep. My wife and I have prayed, opened our doors, and began caring for orphaned and disabled children." I had grown up in the church, been a Christ-follower for two decades, and I had NEVER before heard anyone say, "I can't align myself with the Lord Jesus Christ and not take this action." It was a bold witness that rattled my faith.

I had only met Pastor Raja briefly. I knew he was a humble servant of God. I saw how he was already raising their daughter by faith. I knew he had nothing in His hands to feed these children. At the time, I wondered how these children would survive. This was one of my first examples of audacious generosity. For more than twenty years, I've witnessed the faithfulness of God to miraculously feed, house, educate, and abundantly care for hundreds of children through Raja's home. You should know that Pastor Raja's daughter is now studying in the USA, pursuing her master's degree. This is nothing short of a miracle and evidence of God's faithfulness.

LIVING GENEROUSLY TO GIVE MORE

The time has come for you to open your hands like Pastor Raja and so many others. Bring it on.

CONCLUSION

Congratulations on setting God, yourself, and others free! You are now empowered for limitless giving! Audacious Generosity is what few want, but everybody needs. It's the life you've always wanted. Now your life can be filled with a sense of completeness, satisfaction, and excitement.

SET GOD FREE

In order to enjoy a life of audacious generosity, we worked tirelessly through three steps. First, we had to **set God free**. We did that by daily asking God for more, acknowledging that this will take a lifetime of courage, and accepting God's request to take courage.

SET YOURSELF FREE

Second, we had to **set ourselves free**. We did that by

winning against three boxing matches that keep us from audacious generosity: fear versus freedom, working versus resting, and reprimand versus reward.

SET OTHERS FREE

And third, we had to **set others free**. We did that by flipping the switch from getting more to giving more, from greed to generosity, and from burden to blessing.

Now you are free to live recklessly for God, expectantly from God, and generously for God. I'm so excited for you! God will continue to combine courage and freedom you have begun to experience through audacious generosity. I encourage you to wake up every day excited to become more generous as God gives through you.

LIVING RECKLESSLY FOR GOD

Considering the needs of others beyond your own needs is going to feel absolutely reckless at times. Do it, anyway. God is so confident of His love and care for you that He will ask you to abandon everything for the sake of the call. Now you know this isn't a subtraction from His blessings to you. This is a multiplication of His blessings through you. Living recklessly for God empowers you for limitless giving. That's audacious generosity!

LIVING EXPECTANTLY FOR GOD

I wish someone would have encouraged me to let God change my expectations. I heard about the need to let God change my heart, mind, and habits. I've heard over and over the need to have faith or the need to put my hope in God. But no one has ever encouraged me to let God change my expectations. Now you know that expectations matter. Now you see the power of celebrating in advance. Living expectantly from God empowers you for limitless giving. That's audacious generosity!

LIVING GENEROUSLY FOR GOD

You now understand how much meaning and impact you are about to experience as you live openhandedly before God. Wake up every morning excited to become more generous as God gives through you. When it comes to giving, do it and do it out of love. He is worthy of your everything! Honor God, and He will honor His Word. You can never outgive God. Living generously for God empowers you for limitless giving. That's audacious generosity!

THE KEY IS GOD'S PRESENCE

We focused a lot on John 6 and the miracle of the Feeding of the Multitude. Pastor Steven Furtick of Elevation Church says it was the disciples' close proximity to Jesus that enabled them to experience the miracle. I encourage you to passionately pursue the presence of God first and foremost in your life. You now know that is the key to audacious generosity. As soon as you wake up tomorrow, I want you to immediately ask God for more. Then do it again the next day, and the next.

GET READY FOR MIRACLES

God's Word is filled with accounts of God filling His people's hands for His mission. We see it in the Old Testament as God fills Noah's hands (Genesis 6), Sarah's hands (Genesis 21), Moses' hands (Exodus 14), and David's hands (1 Samuel 17) for His mission—just to name a few. We see it in the New Testament as God fills the disciples' hands (John 6), Jesus' hands (John 19), Peter and John's hands (Acts 8), and Paul's hands (Acts 19) for His mission—again, just to name a few (it happens a lot!).

God's mission has always been to give us the gift of His presence. God has always been the Giver. Giving has always depended on RELEASING what He puts into our hands. Today we see God fill our hands for His mission. Jesus has no confusion about us being his hands on the earth. You and I shouldn't, either.

FULFILLING THE GREAT COMMISSION

In Revelation 7:9-12, God reveals where we are headed.

This is what fulfilling the Great Commission looks like. In Matthew 24:14, Jesus promises, "This gospel of the kingdom will be preached in the whole world as a testimony to all nations, and then the end will come," (NIV).

Audacious generosity is a movement in which Believers around the world unite to fulfill the Great Commission. It is you, me, and every Believer saying, "Lord, Here am I. Send me." It is you, me, and every Believer saying, "Here are my hands. Fill them for the Great Commission." It is not just believing that everyone ought to have access to hear about Jesus. It is taking action to do something about it as God works in and through you to accomplish His mission.

This is how the mission and strategy transferred from Jesus to the disciples and from the disciples to Paul and leaders of the early Church. This is how it is transferred to me and to you. This is how God transfers it to others. Many people have become involved in the Great Commission because they committed to what I had committed to. Now it is time for others to get involved in the Great Commission because of what you have committed to. This is how God will continue until Matthew 24:14 is fulfilled.

The hour has come for you to unite with Believers standing side-by-side and locked arm-in-arm around the world to fulfill the Great Commission. God has united you with precious Believers around the world. God has united you with beautiful brothers and sisters in Christ. The world desperately needs your unique piece of this movement, and God is ready to fill your hands for His mission.

The time has come for you to join the movement. My prayer is that you can enjoy a living relationship with God that's fueled by courage, characterized by freedom, and overflowing with audacious generosity. As God combines courage and freedom in your life, you will experience, receive, and give more than you ever thought possible.

You are ready. You are not alone.

Open your hands.

PSALM 67

May God be merciful and bless us.
May his face smile with favor on us.
May your ways be known throughout the earth,
your saving power among people everywhere.
May the nations praise you, O God.
Yes, may all the nations praise you.
Let the whole world sing for joy,
because you govern the nations with justice
and guide the people of the whole world.
May the nations praise you, O God.
Yes, may all the nations praise you.
Then the earth will yield its harvests,
and God, our God, will richly bless us.
Yes, God will bless us,
and people all over the world will fear him.

AVAILABLE

BY ELEVATION WORSHIP

Narrow as the road may seem
I'll follow where your spirit leads
Broken as my life may be
I will give You every piece
Chorus:
I hear You call
I am available
I say yes Lord
I am available
Here I am with open hands
Counting on Your grace again
Less of me and more of You
I just wanna see You move
Chorus

Here I am, here I am
You can have it all
You can have it all
Here I am, here I am
You can have it all
You can have it all
For the one who gave me life
Nothing is a sacrifice
Use me how you want to God
Have your throne within my heart

SONGWRITERS:

BEN FIELDING, CHRISTOPHER JOEL BROWN, JASON
INGRAM, MATTHEW REDMAN, STEVEN FURTICK

$25,000
GENEROSITY AWARD

Looking for The World's Best Story of Audacious Generosity

GREAT STORIES DEMONSTRATE:

1 Generosity **2** Courage **3** Impact

ANNUAL TIMELINE:

- February 15 - 100 semi-finalists chosen
- April 1 - 10 finalists chosen
- May 25 - 1 winner awarded $25,000

Find Samples and Submit Stories at:
kevinwhite.us

ACKNOWLEDGMENTS

To Shelly, Zach, Brittany, Kourtney, and Kali, I can't thank God enough for you. Thank you for your willingness to live out audacious generosity with me.

I want to thank each member of the board of directors of Global Hope India throughout the years. I will never forget how each of the current members individually prayed over me as I wrote this book. I also thank our Indian partners and pastors in India who encouraged me and prayed fervently for me as I wrote.

I thank the men of God who believed in me and poured into me at various moments during my life: Pastor Danny Janes, Rev. Hank Williams, Dr. Jim Bross, Dr. Bob Black, Dr. John Maxwell, Pastor Mike Ennis, Don Oglesby, Pastor Ross DeMerchant, Dr. Marlin Mull, Dr. Keith Carroll, Joe

Thompson, Tom Gould, Pastor Raja Kumar Partap, Pastor Ricky Mills, Pastor Mike Lee, Pastor Dave Patchin, Dr. Gary Vet, Pastor Jay Reynolds, Pastor JD Greear, Jonathan Gould, Justin Keishing, Pastor Matt Bush, Chris Thompson, Chad Langhoff, Dr James Jernigan, Matthew Farwell and Pastors Claude Thomas and Jesse Coquoz. There are many others. I thank each of you for pointing me toward Jesus.

God used a lot of people to turn this book into a reality. Thank you Bart Queen for your coaching through the manuscript. Thank you Dr. Gary Vet and Dr. Doug Hilliard for your reviews and feedback. Thank you Holly, Thomas, and Jennifer for helping with grammar. I appreciate everyone who prayed, encouraged, and offered feedback as I wrote.

Finally, huge thanks to the magnificent team at Scribe Publishing for your excellent support and services.

THANK YOU BACKERS

This book about miracles depended on a miracle from God to be published. Thank you to everyone who backed the Kickstarter project that turned this book into a reality.

Ayo and Abiola Adeyefa	Stephanie Jameson	Sabin Shrestha
Saurabh Animesh	Andrew Jarman	Joshua Solapuri
Jim Anthony	James and Brianne Jernigan	Peter Somai
Jennifer Allen	Johnathan Kraus	Peyton and Brittany Spivey
Ellie Argaluza	Chihanpam Keishing	Stephen
Chris and Rebecca Ayers	Justin Keishing	Houston Stephens
Jim and Mary Ayers	Pemthingchon Keishing	Hunter Stricklin
Pamyui Awungshi	Worchipem Keishing	Stephen and Amanda Superville
Phil and Ann Bailey	Raj and Sowmya Kiran	Derek and Erin Taylor
Pastor Sebastian Bernardshaw	Dr. Chakravarthy and Shabina Koonapareddy	Chris and BJ Thompson

Ronald and Deshika Bethune

Brian and Deidra Blackmore

Melody Bowes

Deborah Bradshaw

Matt and Sarah Bush

Valerie Carlson

Pastor Pongom Chai

Diane Cook

Jesse and Danielle Coquoz

Paul and Heather Corbett

Scott Coring

Raja Chuttugalla

Dave and Susie Demski

Prabhu and Jessica Dondapati

LaDonna Earwood

Mac and Gail Ellis

Matthew and Teslin Farwell

Dave and Joanie Fordice

Debra Forrester

Priscilla Fraire

Emma Getz

Jessica Hook

Irving

Pastor Raja and Sree Kumar

Chad and Amber Langhoff

Tom and Barb Lepkowski

Wendy Luong

Manoj and Priya Magar

Ken and Anita Martin

Brandon McCarrell

Valerie McConnell

John and Viola Messiah

Pauline Miller

Kimberly Miner

Haley Modlin

Charles and Jennifer Moretz

David and Bethany Morgan

Dan and Nancy Nelson

Jackie Nelson

Christine Nyambura

Andre Peres

Kyle and Jenn Rasmussen

Rachel Royster

Ryan and Lisa Sack

Pastor Polsapalli & Sharon Sekhar

Clint and Jenny Tillerson

David and Jennie Tran

Sam and Nancy Volk

David and Charlotte Watson

Patti Weisner

Jonathan and Donna White

Kali White

Kourtney White

Shelly White

Zach and Brittany White

Kirk and Wendy Willard

David and Amanda Williams

Ben Wilson

Jay and Liz Reynolds

Nelson Rha

Dave and Sarah Beth Richardson

Bethany Royster

Leisa Royster

Jonathan and Christy Gould

Tom Hickman

Steven and Becky Holley

Jim and Yvonne Schaefer

ADVANCE PRAISE FOR
AUDACIOUS GENEROSITY

After finding my identity and freedom in Christ, my concept of Stewardship has been governed by two simple principles: "Never deny a generous impulse" and "You can't outgive God." Audacious Generosity is simply extending to others what God has given to us. Kevin didn't seek to be generous, he sought the Lord and His presence. The result is a ministry that exceeded his expectations. Audacious Generosity is a treasure for those seeking to discover their potential to be all that God created them to be.

—DR. NEIL T. ANDERSON, FOUNDER AND PRESIDENT
EMERITUS, FREEDOM IN CHRIST MINISTRIES

Read Audacious Generosity only if you are willing to risk being transformed by God. No matter where you are today, Auda-

cious Generosity can be the springboard launching you into being a person who would bless the nations.

In this compelling, practical, and easy-to-read book, Kevin shares from his personal experience of how God transformed someone with absolutely no hope for a future into a person who is passionately inspiring people around the world to experience abundant life in Christ. I dare you not to miss the opportunity of impacting millions in this world by understanding your unique role in fulfilling the great commission.

—DR. ANIL BENJAMIN, PHYSICIAN, SHALOM MEDICAL CENTRE, PRESIDENT, BRIDGE OF HOPE, INDIA

The title Audacious Generosity is so Kevin. I have been associated with Kevin White since 2013, and I know him to be the most generous and selfless person, generous without a fault! I can vouch that every page resounds that testimony. I will recommend everyone to grab a copy and read it. Audacious Generosity will inspire you, challenge you, and ignite the joy of giving in you.

—REV. ACHU CHANG, EXECUTIVE SECRETARY, CHANG BAPTIST CHURCHES ASSOCIATION, NAGALAND, INDIA

I'm thankful to be a coworker and friend with Kevin White since 2015. I've witnessed with my own eyes the power of generosity through Kevin. I'm excited about the impact of Audacious Generosity. Not only will Audacious Generosity change your

life, but it will change the lives of millions impacted by God's generosity through you.

—JUSTIN KEISHING, INTERNATIONAL TRAVEL MANAGER, GLOBAL HOPE INDIA, MANIPUR, INDIA

As a coach of spoken communication for over thirty years, my ultimate goal with anyone I coach is to "LET THEIR LIFE SPEAK." Not just their words. Not just their actions. It is when their words and their actions are inseparable! Kevin White is a great example of "Letting your life speak." Kevin is a LIVING example of Audacious Generosity. When it comes to living out the principle of Audacious Generosity, he is the proof and the definition. If you doubt in any small way that God can't use you in extraordinary ways, read Kevin's journey of Audacious Generosity. Kevin has transformed how I see giving and what God can do through my ordinary hands. Audacious Generosity is my ordinary hands being used by an Extraordinary God! Kevin shows the way!

—BART QUEEN, CEO AND FOUNDER, SPEAK AMERICA

Pastor Kevin White has an ability to speak straight to your soul. Just being around him draws me into a closer relationship with Christ. God is on the move and is raising up those who fully embrace His love, power, and authority to do the impossible. Audacious Generosity will transform the trajectory of your life in all the best ways.

—DR. JAMES JERNIGAN, CORNERSTONE CHIROPRACTIC

I have not only witnessed, but experienced how Kevin lives a life of audacious generosity. Whether it is his time, money, or any other resource, Kevin uses it to raise up those around him. He has taught me that generosity doesn't come from abundance, but abundance is a result of generosity. Reading this book will show you how you can start living a life of audacious generosity TODAY!

—JESSE COQUOZ, GUEST EXPERIENCE DIRECTOR, ELEVATION CHURCH MORRISVILLE

Kevin White is a man who believes in the life-transforming power of Jesus Christ. Why? Because his life has been transformed by the power of Jesus, and his life is dedicated to helping others experience that same power. Accept Kevin's invitation to see and experience the presence of God like you have never seen before.

—KEN MARTIN, CPA, STANCIL PUBLIC ACCOUNTING, MEMBER, BOARD OF DIRECTORS, GLOBAL HOPE INDIA

I have known Kevin for over ten years. He introduced us to missions in India. My husband and I have been involved ever since through Global Hope India. I have seen Kevin's commitment to God's calling to India and his God-given compassion for the people of India. The stories, experiences, and lessons in Audacious Generosity should be an encouragement to anyone seeking the courage to live out God's calling in their life and learn as Kevin has to always ask God for more.

—REBECCA S. AYERS, PHD, VICE PRESIDENT, BOARD OF DIRECTORS, GLOBAL HOPE INDIA

I met Kevin White during his first trip to India in 1998. We have been friends ever since. He is the right man to write this book. His life is an example of the title. Not only for the teachings but because his life is a model for generosity. I have experienced the blessings of God's love, compassion, and empathy even in days of crisis through Kevin's generosity. I have seen Jesus and walked under the shadow of God's love through Kevin.

—PASTOR RAJA PARTAP KUMAR, HYDERABAD FULL
GOSPEL FELLOWSHIP MINISTRIES, HYDERABAD, INDIA

It's been a joy to know Kevin White for the last seven years and his deep desire and commitment to impact India for Christ. He has done this by empowering indigenous ministries. Audacious Generosity is not so much about funding, or how much you can give, but how we can impact nations with a generous mindset with what God has entrusted to us.

—DR. SAJI K. JOHN, THE JOHN
FOUNDATION, HYDERABAD, INDIA

Kevin White has been a good friend to me for six years. He's a true leader and partner in the ministry. I praise God for the desire and vision God put on his heart to write a book on generosity. It's a topic Kevin has personally experienced and lived. I can boldly confess that I don't see any other person appropriate to write a book on audacious generosity other than Kevin. I've learned many things about generosity through him. He is my role model for generosity. He has been sharing life and everything he has with others. I strongly recommend everyone get copies of this Holy Spirit inspired, life-changing, and mind-transforming book. Your life will never be the same, and you will be immensely blessed as you read *Audacious Generosity*.

—PASTOR SEBASTIAN BERNARDSHAW, CHURCH
OF THE WORD, CHENNAI, INDIA

Kevin White is inspirational and a true leader! After knowing Kevin for three years and traveling with him across the globe, I can truly say that I have never met a more selfless and dedicated man! His passion to serve others and make a difference in the world around him is both encouraging and energizing. Kevin leads by example and has the courage and compassion to make this world a better place!

—CHRIS THOMPSON, BOARD OF DIRECTORS,
GLOBAL HOPE INDIA (FELLOW VOLUNTEER
AT ELEVATION CHURCH MORRISVILLE)

Kevin is a longtime friend who is passionate about engaging the church for the glory of God. He exercises his calling pouring out his life to see the church of Christ on fire for reaching the lost in the world. His desire in this book is to see the people of God awaken to the mighty power of God, and live lives of generosity, availing themselves to the real, personal, and transformational work of the Holy Spirit. This book will equip and encourage you to see, know, and experience more of God as you follow Christ's example of Audacious Generosity.

—JOSH BECK, PRESIDENT, BOARD OF
DIRECTORS, GLOBAL HOPE INDIA

Pastor Kevin White and I met in God's providence in May 2016. It turned out to be a divine connection. Kevin is a very good friend to me and my wife. He is a caring, committed, and generous person. I wholeheartedly recommend his book, Audacious Generosity, as he indeed walks the talk!

—PASTOR MANOJ MAGAR, RAYS OF HOPE, INDIA

WEEKLY PODCAST BY KEVIN WHITE

Subscribe
KEVINWHITE.US

The Audacious Generosity Podcast with Kevin White empowers listeners world-wide for limitless giving. Kevin showcases heart-warming stories of people from around the world as God works through them with audacious generosity to fulfill His mission. Subscribe now for your weekly dose of encouragement and discover how to experience, receive and give more than you ever thought possible.

WEEKLY PODCAST BY KEVIN WHITE

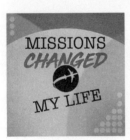

Subscribe
KEVINWHITE.US

Here comes your weekly dose of courage for the missionary in all of us. Buckle up! You're going to hear amazing stories of radical transformation by actual mission trip participants from around the world. Every episode includes an inspiring word from God crafted just for you! We take you right inside 20+ years of real life mission trip devotional moments in India. If that is not enough, every week we share practical tools to empower you as God uses missions to change your life.

GLOBALHOPEINDIA.ORG

Helping you **make Christ known** among people with **limited ACCESS** to hear about **Jesus**

3 WAYS TO ENGAGE:

Pray	**Give**	**Go**
Stand in the Gap	Share Funds	Send People
Ezekiel 22:30	Luke 16:9	Mark 16:15
We empower you to stand in the gap through prayer. We believe when we pray God works.	We empower you to give financially to strengthen The Church in India in their outreach of the gospel.	We empower you to go or send people on short-term mission trips to India.

20 YEARS - THOUSANDS OF SALVATIONS:

1 Baptisms **2** Pastors Trained **3** New Churches Launched

Because everyone should have **ACCESS** to hear about Jesus

ABOUT THE AUTHOR

Over twenty years ago, **KEVIN WHITE** went on his first mission trip to India. He's been staring at the need and opportunity to fulfill the Great Commission ever since.

Kevin is the Founder/Executive Director of Global Hope India, a mission organization providing access to the gospel to Indian Nationals. He's now traveled to India over fifty times, hosting a thousand people on mission trips.

Kevin and his wife, Shelly, have three adult children and one grandchild. They live in Cary, North Carolina.